FIRST EDITION

YO-AFP-008

I'M GLAD I LOOK LIKE A TERRORIST

Growing Up Arab in America

BY RAY HANANIA

Urban Strategies Group Publishing Inc.
Tinley Park, Illinois

I'M GLAD I LOOK LIKE A TERRORIST: GROWING UP ARAB IN AMERICA

Requests for Information should be sent to:

Urban Strategies Group Publishing Inc.
PO Box 356
Tinley Park IL 60477
708-403-3380
FAX: 708-403-3380
BBS: 708-429-0553
E-mail: **rhanania@theramp.net**
Web: **http://www.usg.org**

Printed in the United States of America.
ISBN: 0-9654761-0-3

Acknowledgements

This book is dedicated to Carolyn Ann Haifa Hanania. Be proud of your heritage, your people and yourself.

It is also dedicated to Assad and Lillian Shorrosh, Fawzi and Sonia Kronfil, Issa Kronfil, Janet Canahuati, Leila al-Hin, Yousef Tarud and family, Nick and Shirley Khoury, and especially to my sister Linda and to my brother John.

Without all of them, growing up would have been impossible.

There are many others who helped by supporting me during many of the events detailed in this book. Without them, these stories could not be told.

They include Jim Zogby and Casey Kasem who offered advice and support on leadership and community involvement.

I want to thank Professor Ibrahim Abu-Lughod, who always provided guidance and support to members of his community, was always an inspiration and role model to me personally. Professor Abu-Lughod's role as a Palestinian American leader helped bring our people together.

Community leaders like Rouhy Shalabi, Talat Othman, Sam Zanayed, Hasan Al-Khatib, Ayoub and Ghada Talhami, Samir Khalil, Khalil Shalabi, Suheil Nammari, Miriam Zayed and Faisal Muhammad have all worked unselfishly for the best interests of our community, and were there to make my election campaign, which is a part of this book, financially successful.

The Rev. Fr. Nicholas Dahdal of St. George Church always offered inspiration, and his predecessor, Fr. Anatasios Emert is fondly remembered as a close family friend.

Fadi Zanayed, Fuad Ateyeh, Adnan Saleh, Jamal Al-Nisr, Abdullah Wajeeh and members of the Palestinian American Congress, who supported my candidacy as National President and who are intensely involved in the work of the PAC, are due gratitude.

I also want to thank Albert Mokhiber of the AAUG, Jeryl Levin of the Illinois Ethnic Coalition and Jonathan Levine of the American Jewish Committee, all for their words of support and friendship during some of the events of the enclosed essays.

These are all among a rare collection of leaders who work for the benefits of their communities more than they do for themselves.

I would like to also express my sincere gratitude to both the *Daily Southtown Economist Newspaper*, where I learned how to write, and especially to the current editors and the staff of the Chicago *Sun-Times*, where I learned to love the journalism profession. Remembrances included in this collection that touch upon my years at the Chicago *Sun-Times* are related with affection and respect.

And, I especially want to thank Tony Rezko, a truly dedicated Arab American whose generous encouragement helped make this book possible.

Ray Hanania
Orland Park, Illinois
October, 1996

Preface

Ask not what your country can do for you.
Ask what you can do for your country ...

If you lived through the American 60s, you were an American. How can anyone not call me an American?

I worked at being an American, but I was treated like a foreigner, an alien, a stranger in my own country.

My memories struggle through it as I grow older.

I heard President John F. Kennedy speak the words above at his inauguration, even though I did not learn until more than two decades later that his words were also the words of a great Arabian philosopher and 19th Century writer named Gibran Khalil Gibran.

We didn't learn about him in our schools.

In fact, as a student, Arab role models were not among our curriculum. Few Arabs were presented to us in school as real heros or role models. There wasn't one that I was encouraged to admire.

Still, I was inspired as an American, with a gaping hole in my ethnic heart.

I was there when Kennedy was assassinated, and I know exactly where I was the moment I heard the news: walking up the slight incline of the playground at Joseph Warren Elementary school at 92nd and Jeffery Avenue. A friend had yelled to me, "Did you hear that the president was killed?"

No, I said.

And frankly, after Kennedy was inaugurated, I had heard little about him, because I was too young.

But, I was not too young to become a part of 20th Century

Americana.

How can anyone not call me an American?

I watched every episode of *Gilligan's Island*. I lived through the great escapades of Batman and Robin. I grew up with Opie Taylor and Andy.

"Can I go outside and play, paw?" I would ask my dad.

I dreamed of Jeannie. I sighed every time Sonny and Cher sang "I Got You Babe" during their television specials.

I shivered at the unknown when we were told that Sputnik was flying above our homes. And, I was excited when on Feb. 20, 1962, John Glenn circled the Earth three times in Friendship 7.

Neighbors named their firstborn after Glenn and other astronauts who helped us to believe in the unbelievable and to visualize our secret fears from the unknowns of outer space.

I sat and watched the agony of the Vietnam war several feet from the luminescent television screen in the comfort of my front room.

And I registered for the draft when I reached the right age.

I witnessed the riots at the Democratic National Convention, and found myself drawn to a Sly and the Family Stones concert that turned into a riot when the musicians' helicopter was denied landing at Grant Park.

How can anyone not call me an American?

I memorized the lyrics to every Jimi Hendrix song, and to the songs of Led Zeppelin, Grand Funk Railroad. They joined a chorus of songs I had engraved in my heart from the Beatles, who inspired me to play lead guitar. I bought a gold Les Paul and jammed out American music in a small band from my garage.

I could play the *Star Spangled Banner*, in protest, with my teeth, and also anchored on the back of my neck.

Music was a common denominator that helped bring people together, though. And, ironically, most Americans learned about rock and roll from a popular radio announcer, Casey Kasem, who I didn't learn was Arab until many years later.

I was there with my dad watching television when Jack Ruby rushed up to Lee Harvey Oswald, shoved his pistol into Oswald's stomach and fired, forever etching the fear of "conspiracy" in my American mind.

I was there at Robert Kennedy's side, cradling his blood soaked head, minutes after a Palestinian Arab immigrant from Jordan had killed him.

Sirhan Sirhan.

That was one time I remember being taught about "Arabs" in school and while watching the TV news.

I didn't cry for Sirhan Sirhan. I felt sorry for him. He was wrong when he claimed that Kennedy was the tool of the Israeli lobby, a chord that rang true in the hearts of many Arab Americans, but could never justify his murderous deed.

I saw the play backs of the minutes that followed in the wake of the murder of the Rev. Martin Luther King Jr. on the balcony of a Memphis motel.

How can anyone not call me an American?

I lived with my parents, and brother and sister, as we all experienced the fears of White Flight during the late 60s and real-estate exploitation and neighborhood panic-peddling.

These were not simply terms that could be learned from a book.

If you lived through the 60s, you were American.

The world continued to change and television continued to help us experience these moments throughout the 70s and 80s that followed.

Tears welled up in my eyes as we watched over and over again, the footage of the Challenger exploding 73 seconds after lift-off. We had seen so many perfect launchings from the Kennedy Space Center, that they had become routine and the dangers forgotten.

I never did know until many years later that one of the seven crew members, Christa McAuliffe, was an Arab American herself.

It was a moment of pride we were denied.

I cried when John Lennon was murdered. And I remember

watching his first performance of *Day Tripper* on the *Ed Sullivan Show*, sitting on the rug covered wood floor in a small apartment of another Arab American family, huddled with my parents apart from society because we felt different from the rest.

Lennon had angered my parents when he said somewhat innocently that the Beatles were "more popular" than Jesus Christ.

How could that be to my relatives who lived in the Caribbean, South America and the Middle East? They were shocked and angered. To them, Lennon symbolized American decadence and immorality.

What would they have said if they had heard the lyrics of Frank Zappa, and knew that he was Arab too?

I grew up Arab in a polarized America.

These same experiences could not bring me closer to Americans. Despite our loyalty and our experiences, Arab Americans always felt different, outsiders, from the rest of American society.

This book is not simply about growing up Arab in America. It is about growing up American as an Arab, in a country that could be both charitable and cruel to foreigners and to "unacceptable" ethnics like myself.

It is about ethnicity in America, from an Arab perspective.

We pushed our ethnicity down because we wanted dearly to be a part of this country. We changed our names, gave ourselves nicknames, to make it easier for Americans to accept us.

Kaffirs, or sub-humans.

Discriminated against.

Victims of bias and stereotyping.

Defenseless against the fears and frustrations of society.

These words have meaning to us.

No one can really understand the truth of their own ethnicity until they have experienced the pains and joys of another's.

In the American melting pot, Arab Americans are a small bubble, an ingredient that still floats apart from the rest of society's brew.

As Americans, we Arabs must accept part of the blame.

As Americans, we all must stir that pot to bring us all together.

Many Arab Americans objected to the name of this book and the use of the word "terrorist," which to many Arabs has become a derogatory word directed at us, about us, and to us.

It was only after the Oklahoma City bombing and the realization that the threat of terrorism does not have an ethnic face that some of the gut reaction that fuels the emotions of the word "terrorist" tempered and caused many in the West to apply caution.

I am not a terrorist.

But to run from the word "terrorist" is wrong.

I am glad I look like a terrorist because it gives me a special sword to help destroy the stereotype that continues to injure my people, distort our image and to cause otherwise compassionate Americans to engage in hateful acts of bias.

Table of Contents

I'm Glad I Look Like a Terrorist

Growing Up Arab in America

By Ray Hanania

*What is written on your forehead,
the eye can read ...*
                        An Arab Saying

You are what you are ...
                        An American saying

Ya Habibi:
An Arab Childhood

My mom wanted me to be a doctor or a grocer, but I never realized that I would someday grow up to be an Arab.

My father, George Hanna Hanania, was born in Jerusalem, the son of a traveling merchant. After he came here in the twenties, he didn't forget his Arab heritage, but he didn't wear it like a chip on his shoulder, either. Dad believed that 'blending in' was the key to a successful life here. Racism and bigotry were forms of ignorance, he would say. Americans fear the unknown; to win them over, you had to become their friend. As easy as it is to hate a stranger, it's hard to hate a friend.

My mother, Georgette Dabdoub Kronfil, was the daughter of a Bethlehem tailor. Her marriage to my father was arranged. Dad was about 45 and mom was 21. They met about one month before the wedding.

Dad insisted that all his children be given American-sounding names. I was named after a doctor in South Shore hospital. As my mother remembered it, she was still under sedation when she heard the nurse paging "Dr. Raymond! Dr. Raymond" on the intercom system. "Doctor" was one of the few words mom knew in English at the time.

I grew up in a predominantly Jewish neighborhood on Chicago's South Side. In fact, many Arabs I knew grew up in predominantly Jewish neighborhoods, because Arabs and Jews actually have much in common. And were it not for the Arab-Israeli wars, we would have had a fine existence together, eating the same foods, sharing the same ties to biblical history (my last name is a Hebrew word that means *God has been Gracious*), and boasting the same kind of overbearing mother.

My own mother didn't suffer as loudly as some, but coming from a poor village, she was incredibly frugal. When I would complain, mom would say *Ya Habibi* ("My love") and remind me about the little refugee children in Palestine who lived in tents with no food or clothing.

So when the other guys were all wearing Gants with "Lucky Loops," I went around dressed in Goldblatt's bargain-basement plaids. "Labels can't keep you warm, *ya habibi*," mom would say.

When my friends sported ducktail haircuts, my hair was cut in a kitchen by mom. "Why spend $3.50 when I can cut it just as good?" She cut it "just as good" until I was 25.

And when I outgrew my shoes, mom took a knife and cut the leather from the front so that my wool-socked toes would stick out. "The sole is still good," she'd say, smiling. "*Ya habibi*, there are kids running around barefoot in *Falusteen!*"

Looking down at my feet, I envied them.

Arab mothers are great cooks, and mom was no exception. The food was hot and spicy, and there was always enough of it for 20 people. A typical dinner consisted of *humos*, garbanzo beans mixed with a sesame paste called *tahina*; *falafil*, deep fried bean cakes; *tabouleh*, salads of diced tomato, cucumber, parsley, and cracked wheat; and *labaneh*, yogurt that was poured on nearly everything. Everything was stuffed, from green peppers to zucchini.

I loved it all, except for one thing--okra, the Arab equivalent of spinach. No vegetable got wrapped in a napkin or shoved behind a refrigerator faster than okra. Arabs put it in their rice, stews, salads, and dips. Although my mom always denied it, I'm convinced she used to sneak it into our milk shakes.

My favorite was *wariq duwally*--boiled grape leaves stuffed with cooked rice and lamb and then wrapped like little cigars. Mom kept boxes of plastic bags in the trunk of the car and would make dad pull over every time we drove by a grapevine in a forest preserve or park. She would march us out and we would start picking the leaves, stuffing them into our bags.

Stripped vines along any roadside are a sure sign that you are entering an Arab neighborhood. Of course, if you see women wearing *babushkas* across their faces instead of over their heads, that's another good sign.

Every time I invited a friend over for dinner, mom would cook *wariq duwally*. My friends would tell everyone at school the next day that mom made them eat "little pieces of shit."

My friends didn't have much trouble figuring out that I was a little different. They always wanted to know what my nationality was. "Cereal," I would reply. I thought I was saying "Syrian."

As far as my friends were concerned, I was a Jew, like them. They nicknamed me "Herman," and went out of their way to make me a part of their lives. I spent my early teens hanging around the JCC and Mel Markon's original deli nearby sipping chocolate phosphates. The Hananias were the first Arab family to apply for membership at the Henry Horn Jewish Community Center at 91st and Jeffery Avenue. I don't remember why it didn't work.

One time I even made a guest appearance at the local Hebrew school across the street. My friends thought it would give the rabbi a real jolt to see an Arab sitting in the back of the class.

"Are you *Falusteeni*?" the rabbi asked in Hebrew.

"I am an American, Rabbi," I responded meekly.

He knew I was an Arab before I did.

The best time of any teen's life is supposed to be that summer between eighth grade graduation and high school. It would have been that way for me if the Arabs and Israelis hadn't picked the month of my graduation from Joseph Warren Elementary school -- June 1967 -- to begin what would become the Arab world's most humiliating defeat. Israel's armies raced across the Sinai, the West Bank, the Gaza Strip, and the Golan Heights, captured Jerusalem, and crushed Arab pride. All in six days. It put an unavoidable spotlight on my heritage.

The humiliation was on TV, in the movies, in the newspapers, in magazines, and in school. *Time* magazine published Arab jokes. You couldn't turn on a television set without hearing about the celebrations in the Jewish community, and the humiliation of the Arabs.

At school, classes were recessed for 15 minutes each morning during the war so that Jewish students could collect money for the United Jewish Appeal. There I was, a Palestinian Arab carrying a canister with a picture of Egypt's President Gamal Abdel Nasser (whom the Jewish children knew more about than I did), his hand reaching across the caption, "Give to the United Jewish Appeal."

"Hey, Herman, whose side are you on?" one of my Jewish friends asked. "The Arabs' or the Israelis?" All I could think about was that scene in *Exodus* where the Arab who was friendly to the Jews was killed by his own people, hanging in the public square, a Jewish star carved with a knife into his chest.

Like so many people, I learned about being an Arab from the movies. The movie *Exodus* was the American textbook on the subject. The Arab was the villain, of course. Unshaven and dark skinned, he wore a dress, a towel on his head, and a rope around his waist, and he murdered children ruthlessly. He had a mustache and he looked like my Uncle Fawzi.

In fact, almost every TV or Hollywood Arab terrorist looks like some uncle or aunt or cousin of mine. The scene were Fred Dryer (of TV's *Hunter*) pounces on a gaggle of terrorists in the movie *Death Before Dishonor* looks like an assault on a Hanania family reunion.

Bowen High school and its large minority student body, located on the other side of the viaduct, couldn't have come at a better time. Concerns I had about being accepted were overshadowed by the general fear of the Spanish Lords and the Latin Kings.

By 1970, Arabs had stopped living in Jewish neighborhoods. Most of my Jewish friends moved north to Skokie and Niles. We moved to the Southwest Side where half of the city's Arab population lives.

The hardest part of high school was finding a girl to go out with who satisfied my mom. She always wanted me to marry an Arab girl. I would have, but Arab parents never let you date their daughters. Of course, I could never satisfy the parents of my non-Arab girlfriends either. I'm just what every Irish Catholic father wanted for his daughter, a scrawny-looking, dark-skinned Arab.

After graduation, I went to Northern Illinois University, where I signed up for premed classes and where I heard I was the first Arab ever to survive fraternity rush.

My Theta Chi pledge father gave me a paddle addressed "To the Arab from the Jew!" After two years as social chairman, with all-night parties and poor grades, I dropped out and joined the Air Force ... five months before the start of the 1973 Arab-Israeli War.

My drill instructor in basic training ragged me about being a "sand nigger." "You're too gawd-damn dark to be a honky," he barked, " and too light to be a nigga! So what the hey-all are you?"

I spent two years as a medic answering the big question: "If we go to the Middle East to kick some Arab ass, whose side are you gonna be on, Hanya-han-yana?" The nightmare scene from Exodus kept popping up in my mind.

My best friends in the service were Jews -- because while Americans hated "Ay-rabs," they seemed to hate Jews, too)! They just hated me more.

When the war ended, I got married--though not to an Arab woman. (In fact, I got divorced and I married a second time.) Both times we had typical Arab weddings. The men and the women did variations of belly dances, arms waving, hips swaying, and Arabia music wailing. Much of the time, the Arab men danced among themselves. It's a macho thing. You can see similarities between Arab and Jewish culture at a wedding like this. The Jewish national dance, the *Horah*, and the Palestinian national dance, the *Debka*, look exactly alike ... a frenzied combination of a conga line and the hokey-pokey.

I signed up at the University of Illinois in Chicago and changed my major from pre-med to Middle East studies.

If there is any place in this world that needs a United Nations Emergency Peace Keeping Force, it's at the U. of I. Arab and Jewish students there are at war. That's where my political education as an Arab really began.

Someone at the college obviously had a sense of humor because when they assigned campus activity rooms, they put the Organization of Arab Students in one room, Hillel (the Jewish student group) two rooms away, and the student newspaper, *The Illini*, in the room in the middle.

The goal of both sides was to win the support of the American students. What neither side realized was that the American students just didn't care.

The Jewish students would try to do it by organizing festivals recognizing Israel's independence every May. They'd hold rallies at the Circle Forum, where they would sing folk songs, hold candlelight vigils, recite poetry, hold hands and dance, and eat "Israeli foods" like *wariq duwally*, *falafel*, and *humos*.

The Arab students would do it by organizing "Palestine Day" protests -- marking the day the Israelis took over Palestine -- and surrounding the Jewish students. They waved placards written in Arabic, chanted Marxist slogans, embraced weird organizations, and slung angry epithets at the Jewish students.

The Arabs let their anger and emotion overcome their logic: to this day, Arab activists in Chicago prefer demonstrations at the Daley Plaza to more successful means of appealing to Americans.

I was elected president of the Organization of Arab Students my first year there, and I led my share of protests. I remember one in particular. About 50 of us marched from the Daley Center to the Israeli consulate on Wacker Drive--with a 30-man police escort! When it was over, I used the bullhorn to facetiously thank the police for escorting us. The protest committee reprimanded me. A cop came up and shook my hand.

One month later, another Arab student claimed I was "communicating with the Zionists," a capital offense. I was "too American" and I couldn't speak Arabic: OAS dumped me as president.

I signed up for Arabic classes. The Arabs sat on one side, the Jews sat on the other side, and the "other" students sat in the middle. The teacher was an Iraqi Jew who had a peculiar sense of humor, I thought. Nearly every one of his tests included the one question that no Arab student could ever answer correctly:

"What is the capitol of Israel?" the teacher would ask with a smile.

All the Arabs grumbled and wrote "Tel Aviv."

The answer that got you a passing grade was the answer that started five Middle East wars.

"Jerusalem is the capitol of Israel," the teacher would say in English and then repeat in Arabic, "*Urshalimu, asimatu Israelah.*" There was no such sentence in the Arabic language!

Before I left school, I was elected spokesman for the Arab-American Congress for Palestine, a citywide organization. I also started -- in 1975 -- Chicago's first English - language Arab newspaper, *The Middle Eastern Voice*.

Both gave me access to public forums to espouse my views. They also helped attract the attention of the FBI.

FBI agents interviewed my neighbors, my friends, some teachers and a few relatives for more than two years. It upset me. What right did they have to investigate me? What had I done wrong?

Later, I got a copy of their report. It began by suggesting that I was involved in terrorism, and ended 12 pages later saying I was just a person concerned with "bettering my community."

It was nice to see they drew the distinction.

Arabs are among the most superstitious people in the world.

You will see wooden camels, mother-of-pearl backgammon (*tawlah*) boards, and even a hookah (*arjilah*) in an Arab home. But, you will rarely see a seashell. It's bad luck -- an animal lost its home.

Caged birds are bad luck, too. You think that in their cages they are singing about love, peace, and harmony? They are singing curses at you for locking them up. But a bird flying around in your house is a symbol of good fortune. Just don't kill it.

Don't hang philodendrons in the house. They symbolize the devil's tears. Don't roll your hands around and over each other in rapid motion. It is a symbol of death.

I could deal with most of the superstitions. But I drew the line when I bought my first home. Mom suggested we bring it good luck ... by cutting a pigeon's throat on the front porch. "Everyone did it in *al-Balad* (old country)," she said. "We could always kill a chicken, *ya habibi*, in the backyard if you are ashamed."

"*Shu malak?*" she'd ask in Arabic. "What's the matter with you?"

We finally settled on an Arab Orthodox priest ... to bless the house, that is.

In the late 1970s, I was invited by Irv Kupcinet to appear on a TV forum with Abba Eban, Israel's most eloquent spokesman and former foreign minister.

While Eban was trying to explain the economic union between Belgium, the Netherlands, and Luxembourg, I looked at the camera with puppy eyes, and appealed directly to American sympathies.

Eban was born "Aubrey Solomon" in Cape Town, South Africa. My dad was born in Jerusalem. "How come you can go to Jerusalem anytime you want and become a citizen of Israel, and I can't?" I asked.

Eban was very understanding. He told me he would be happy to take me to Jerusalem. I responded, what about the other three million Ray Hananias? Can they come, too?

Kup, who later became a good friend, was not as understanding. When he asked me what it was that I hoped for myself, I said that when I died, I wanted to be buried in Jerusalem.

"I'm sure we can accommodate that request," Kup said, smiling. When I told Kup later that my daughter's middle name was Haifa, in memory of a Palestinian port city, he wrote me a short note saying he hoped I had a son, whom he was sure I would name Jerusalem.

My parents never understood why I wanted to be a journalist. To them and to most Arabs, journalists are ranked below janitors, undertakers, and Israeli soldiers, in that order. None are held in high esteem.

Arabs dislike reporters. That's because there is no such thing as true journalism in the Middle East when my father was a child.

Arabs hate to admit it, but journalists in the Arab world were synonymous with political hacks, government shills employed by government-controlled newspapers and television and radio stations that are filled with government-controlled propaganda, high with emotion and nearly always wrong.

While the Arabs have stringent controls over their media, so do the Israelis, who impose harsh censorship on the Arab press. They frequently jail Arab reporters, another reason to stay out of the business.

But Milton Rakove, a Jewish political science professor at Circle, liked my writings and took me under his wing. I studied with him for several years and eventually became a City Hall reporter and political columnist for The *Southtown Economist* community newspapers.

"Isn't it better to be a terrorist at City Hall than a terrorist in the Middle East?" Rakove asked.

Actually, though, I don't know which is more dangerous, ducking bullets between sand dunes or dodging Chicago Mayor Jane Byrne's barbs.

I've been called a "camel jockey" only once at City Hall, by a North Side alderman angry with stories I did on his zoning deals. Jane Byrne didn't seem to care about my ethnicity. To her, I was just plain old "scum."

It's odd, I suppose, that I ended up covering politics. As a group, Arab-Americans hate going to the polls.

My mentor, Milton Rakove, understood that being pro-Arab was bad politics, and in his book, *Don't Make No Waves, Don't Back No Losers*, he wrote that aspiring politicians "can always support Israel safely. That may alienate the Arabs, but how many Arabs vote in the city anyway?"

Who would Arab Americans vote for if they did want to vote? For years at Democratic and Republican conventions, the issue was not which candidate supported Israel, but which candidate supported Israel more.

It was only recently that Jesse Jackson taught the Arab American community something everyone else already knew: that influence does not start at the top; it starts at the bottom.

And, as my father taught me long ago, so does racism.

(Published in Chicago Magazine, November, 1988)

The Viaduct of Death

S hots! Vaccinations!
They were the hazard of youth when I was growing up on Chicago's South Side.

I don't really understand why my parents had so much faith in inoculations. Shots were symbols of miracles in the Arab World. Maybe that's why so many Arab mothers want their children to become doctors.

Maybe, too, if they gave their children enough shots, they might some how miraculously turn into doctor material.

Whatever the reason, my parents were always taking us to get shots.

My father always tried to be ingenious about getting my sister and I into the car without letting us know that we were really on our way to the doctor to get our shots.

Just the mention of the word ``shot" or any phonetic similarity would be enough to send my sister Linda and I into a hysterical crying rage.

When I was about 8, I remember my dad taking each of us up in each arm one evening and asking, ``How would you kids like to go for ice cream?"

That was an easy question.

``Yea dad. Let's go." Linda and I yelped in eager response as we jumped up and down with excitement.

Linda, who was one year younger than I, raced me to the black and grey 1959 Dodge that was parked at the curb in front of our two-story Georgian brick house on south Luella Avenue.

We would dive into the back seat as dad would reach out and punch the buttons to start the car--the car was supposed to be an industry miracle. Instead of using a gear shift, dad used buttons on the dash to change gears and to put the car into ``Drive" after turning the ignition key.

Dad was always proud of that car, washing it every week--I think the car was only a few years old at the time and was soon to be traded in for a shiny new Red Rambler four door.

And, what a car that was!

Anyway, Linda and I would argue, yell and scream in the back seat. We were so excited about getting ice cream.

We were also too excited to recognize the early warning signs that might have tipped us off that something was awry. Early warning signs that would have told us that our blissful excursion was really a funeral procession for our worst nightmares.

For example, dad didn't react in the normal way as we fought, yelled and screamed in the back seat. Usually, dad reacted in a monstrous rage, yelling and screaming in Arabic and whipping his right hand over the back seat in a blind drive to smack the first little red cherubic face his opened palm could find.

The roar alone from dad's angry mouth and the gush of the wind from his swift hand movement usually was all it took to seal our mouths for at least the next 30 minutes. But although the hand rarely struck, it always sent shivers and fears pounding into our racing little dumpling hearts.

And, when dad or mom yelled in Arabic. Watch out!

But instead, dad just smiled at us in the rearview mirror as we tossed and tumbled in the back seat. And we beamed back at him grateful for our good fortune, unaware of our fate and certain doom.

And, before we left the house, mom and dad spent a lot of time speaking to each other in Arabic. Smiling at us as we caught their glances.

They always spoke Arabic, but not when they were talking to us. When they talked to us, they spoke in English. Dad wanted us to learn English first, although Linda and I learned later to recognize key Arabic words and phrases.

We knew, for example, when we would be eating okra.

There was also another reason to be concerned, a reason that slipped our minds at the mere mention of ``ice cream.''

It was late in the evening for a drive. About 5 p.m. Dad always got home about 4 p.m., walking from the bus stop at 89th and Jeffery Avenue that brought him home from his job at Sinclair Oil Company in the Loop. He was always too tired when he got home from work to go places with us that quickly.

With his broad brimmed fedora and a thin grey cashmere coat, Dad looked like a mobster from the TV show *The Untouchables*. When dad was tired, dad was tired. But this time, he wasn't ``too tired'' to go for a drive?

There was also another certain giveaway that should have alerted us to our fate. Mom didn't insist that we eat dinner first before going out for ice cream. How stupid could we be? Mom let us eat ice cream *before* dinner? No way. No way.

But yes way.

This night she did. With a smile and an encouraging pat on our heads as we waddled off with dad out of the kitchen exchanging chuckles in Arabic.

How cruel it was.

It was all odd, but not enough to shake our resolve. Eventually, however, that resolve started to wear.

The drive to the nearby Tasty Freeze was taking a little too long, about 25 minutes. That prompted Linda and I to calm down, and quizzically ask each other for reassurance about where we were ``really going.''

We refused to wonder aloud or confirm our worst fears. We knew that if something bad was going to happen, the best way to keep it from happening was to not ask dad. (Arab instinct.)

And if we were wrong, and it was known to happen, we certainly didn't want to give dad any ideas.

As the minutes dragged on, and dad's demeanor seemed to

become more serious, we slowly lost our enthusiasm for ice cream.

Linda and I peered over the back seat in dead silence. Our eyes and ears wide open. Our minds racing to try and remember any clue that we might have missed. Dad was just sitting there in the front seat, smiling at us in the rearview mirror, the car humming at 35 miles per hour down the strange street heading God knew where for a promise of ice cream.

``I want a banana split,'' my sister huffed, trying to console us both.

How could she be so cold and uncaring at this moment?

Another sure sign that we were in trouble occurred to us late as we whispered and huddled together docile in the back seat looking like two orphans at Ellis Island.

``If we're going for ice cream, Raymond,'' Linda would ask, ``how come dad didn't ask mom to come along?''

Why was it that my younger sister would always come up with the good question? But I wasn't about to ask dad that either.

So we started searching, searching for clues to our destiny. To confirm our worst fears. And we found it. As the grey Dodge slowly made its final turn to the health clinic it had to pass "The Viaduct of Death."

The Viaduct of Death was a large tunnel with broad letters and symbols painted on its rough cement walls and pillars. Across the top were railroad tracks. But Linda and I never saw a train.

Inside, the tunnel glowed with the dimmed light of yellow street lamps covered with metal cages. Half of the lamps were broken. The street dipped and separated from the sidewalk and curbs which remained at car top level as we entered the Viaduct. The sidewalk was guarded by a black metal railing, railings that looked so strange and ominous.

It was a scene we never forgot, from the first moment we saw it. And the last time we saw it. And that was about a year ago when dad tricked us into getting our annual Polio vaccinations. What was it this time?

Linda was always the first to pale as the car slowly drove through the dark recesses of The Viaduct of Death.

I quickly turned pale green too! But my body started to experience The Viaduct of Death metamorphosis.

My right hand began the transition. Shaking at first erratically and then buzzing at a steady hum, my hand became uncontrollable, jarring my shoulder and making my mind quake with growing fear.

Dad soon caught on as he watched his two children changing before his eyes from normal young kids to animal like vibrators squatting in the back seat, like dogs with uncontrollable flea problems.

Large bubbles of water quickly welled up and filled our eyes, and our lower lips finally gave way and started quivering too. Our lower jaws rattled.

We were in hysterics as dad pulled up to the curb. Dad knew that he'd better get us there quickly before we exploded into millions of little pieces and ear shattering screams.

By the time the car stopped, we were bawling our eyes out. Tears were jumping from our eyes as we marched to our doom, led by a forceful grip from each of my father's hands, tugging us at first and then literally dragging us into the waiting room of the clinic.

The doctor knew the symptoms and tried to buy us off with a cheap little candy sucker wrapped in clear plastic. It wasn't even the good kind and it never worked. But, even in our moments of suffering, we couldn't lose our greed, and we clutched the bribes nonetheless hoping that if we lived through this horror we might find some solace in the sweet candy.

Two nurses would try to still us as the doctor turned toward the white counter top where silver and glass containers clustered in a macabre array at eye level. In the room was the dreaded Big Bed covered by a white paper sheet that pulled out from underneath so that the remnants of blood left by prior victims could not be seen by the next poor, unsuspecting souls.

Nearby, in a corner of the examining room, stood the skeletal remains of some poor youngster who didn't survive the shot. And they said it never hurt anyone.

When the doctor in his white smock turned around, only one hand was visible. The other remained stealthily behind his back with the ``Sterile'' instrument. Soon that giant needle would be piercing our skin as we kicked, screamed and struggled.

Of course, the pain was never as great as we imagined. But, imagination can be very painful.

The needles were actually very small. The nurses pinched our skins as they prepared to give us the shots. The doctor wouldn't stop talking, trying to reassure us that we wouldn't feel a thing.

``Then .... why ... why ... whyyy ... do ... do .. doooo ... we ... we ... weeee ... hab ... hab ... habbbb ... to ....''

In shear sympathy with my unnatural stutter, the doctor would simply pinch my arm more and dive in with the weapon, pulling his hand back quickly and causing my yelping to abruptly halt.

My eyes opened wide and I looked at the doctor and my dad, and also at my sister who was already tugging at dad's sleeve--she had taken the shot first.

It was over in a flash.

``Can we go get ice cream now daddy?'' I asked.

``Why not?'' was dad's reply.

I'm Glad I Look Like a Terrorist

An American Christmas: The Tree

D ad stood there in the lot looking over the selection.

"That one dad," I nudged.

Dad just ignored me on major decisions, and always patronized me when he wanted to show he cared.

"Take it easy, Ray. We'll find a good one," dad said confidently.

Picking out a Christmas tree is no easy matter.

It requires a keen sense of tradition, and a sharp eye.

And, it also takes a few bucks, some real preparation and a real commitment to return to the old values that Christmas represents for most Americans.

This was one of the few times we actually picked out a Christmas tree.

There they all were, displayed at an empty lot on Stony Island Avenue, next to several large semi-trailers I assumed had driven down to Chicago from the North Pole.

The sign on the trucks read "Santa's Xmas Tree Selections."

Most Christmases, we had a fake tree, although you didn't call it fake back in the 60s. It was the fad. Steel and aluminum trees were quite popular in South Shore Valley where we lived on Chicago's South East Side.

"That one dad," I pointed, picking out the tallest tree on the lot.

Dad just kept scanning until his eyes set on a tree that was gigantic. The branches were spread out all over the place, in an even circular movement around the tree.

I kept watching dad's expression for that very moment, and when I caught his glimpse fix in one direction, I knew we had our tree.

"That's it, Ray. That's it."

My brother's name was Johnnie -- every kid in the late 40s and early 50s was named Johnnie. I was named after the doctor that delivered me.

Well, Johnnie just didn't care about the tree as much as I did. A tree was a tree. Someplace where you found presents on Christmas Eve. It was the focal point of the whole celebration, after you finished with church, visiting the relatives, eating dinner, and wearing crisply pressed black suits and stiff-collared white shirts and ties that snapped on over the top neck button.

Johnnie just walked around checking the lot out.

"That guys a drug dealer," he whispered to me, pointing to one of the guys who loaded up the trees and put them in your car. "Watch him, he looks nuts."

Back in those days, anyone with long hair was considered a drug dealer. And, long hair meant anything touching your ear. Being Arab American, if my parents couldn't see a little of my scalp through my hair, it was too long!

The guy who loaded the trees was sucking on a cigar that had long died, and his face was blackened like those soldiers we saw on the Cronkite Show fighting in some strange place called V ... Et ... Nam.

"Drug dealer?" I asked dad. Dad just looked at Johnnie and Johnnie just shrugged.

"Get to the car."

"The car" was a bright red Rambler. Not a Corvette, but in the late 60s, it was just as spectacular. $1,495, I think, is what it cost, a staggering amount for a car back them. It replaced the old black and grey Dodge with the big rear fins, push-button gears, and circular, tube-like front end.

The Rambler had more room than the Dodge, but the tree was still a challenge.

Dad had brought along the rope, blankets and even emptied out the trunk of the spare tire. No one had heard of a bungee cord.

Still wasn't enough room, though.

We put it in tree-trunk first, with the single, weak top branch hanging out the open trunk, the entire tree wrapped several ties with rope and laid on a blanket placed over the trunk lip.

Couldn't scratch that Rambler, even for Christmas!

Back home, mom had the cocoa heating on the stove. She had marshmallows and even made dinner for the occasion: typical Palestinian Arab food, stuffed grape leaves, cracked wheat salad and diced tomatoes and cucumbers, and lamb.

But she had already prepared the small front room in our home on Luella Avenue. The coffee table that used to be in front of the big picture window was gone, and replaced with a red circular floor blanket and a red metal tree holder. The carved olive-wood camels were moved to another location, with the mother-of-pearl curio of the Last Supper.

Four colored flood lights that came with the aluminum tree we normally displayed and that was stored in pieces in the box in the garage circled the spot where the heavy aromad Christmas tree was going to rest.

Needles dropped everywhere, all over the frontroom carpets. It was my job to pick them up.

Johnnie and dad grabbed the tree carefully and centered it over the metal floor holder. Mom filled the container with water mixed with sugar and lemon juice -- supposedly gave the tree stronger aroma.

All I could do was identify the bulb boxes. "Italian" lights were bunched up in a pile nearby, but soon would circle the tree.

When it was together, it was quite a sight.

But all I could do back then was try and guess what was in the long, gift wrapped box that mom thought she had hid successfully in her bedroom closet for "Santa Claus" to deliver.

I knew it was something big.

You didn't put up such a grand tree unless your parents were planning a really cool Christmas.

A Close Shave

Every Arab mother loves to cut their son's hair.

In fact, I think they tried to have young boys just so that they could cut their hair. In 16 years, I know my sister only cut her hair twice.

My friends got their hair cut the old fashioned way.

They went to a barber.

I know, because I used to go with them and watch.

Back in the early 60s, barbers were not the same as hair stylists that we use today. Coiffures were for women. A barber was for a man.

They sat us in the high chair, covered with a white sheet with thin light blue lines.

And the barber talked about sports as he used his scissor to trim my friend's hair. Snip by snip. Clip by clip.

The shears were for cleaning the neck.

And, when they were done, the barber left a little "duck tail" in the back, a kind of signature of "coolness" like the label of a good shirt.

I tried to explain to my mom what a "duck tail" was, but she never did catch on.

One time, she tried, and it looked like a widow's peak, or the front snag of hair on Eddie Munster.

No, mom's hair cutting style was a little different than the barber.

She loved to use the shears. It was American.

Mom must have loved being an American because she loved all the gadgets that came with citizenship. The hair shears. The Osterizer. The vacuum cleaner. The air conditioner. The TV and soaps. My mom knew Loretta Young better than the neighbors.

If my mom struggled in the kitchen, certainly she enjoyed it.

And the Osterizer made that work her joy.

In it went all the leftovers, from carrots to peas and juices. You see, mom didn't just watch American TV. She lived it. All her understandings came from her family, her neighbors and the world of television.

The Osterizer was a part of that culture, and she learned how to juice every morsel of leftovers in that gadget.

The hair shears was another on-TV experience that she embraced.

But, she also loved to use the bowl when cutting my hair. At least at first. It offered an even cut. It was simple. Who would see me sitting in the kitchen, wrapped in a white sheet, hair splashed around me on the tile floor, and the bowl on my head?

I couldn't stop her from using the bowl immediately, although as I neared my teens either she got tired of my complaining or she simply got better and didn't need it.

But when I was young, the bowl provided a good measure for a clean, smooth trim around your head.

She would always leave bangs in the front like the Beatles. But never enough hair so that I could brush it across my face like my friends did.

She thought the Beatles were "cute." Until John Lennon insulted the entire Christian World by claiming that he was more popular "than Jesus Christ."

That was it. He became the devil over night. It didn't stop me from humming their early songs as mom's shears buzzed away around my ears, across my forehead and along the sides.

You could always see the skin on the sides of my head. And she always managed to over cut the hair around my ears. White walls took on new meaning around my ears, which were already big and stuck out like antennas.

Mom did everyone's hair. Dad's. Johns. And mine. And *Untar*, the dog. Err, the over-pampered poodle. He got his hair cut with the shears, too. (*Untar* is the name of an Arab prince, and five of our dogs.)

You could almost pick out all the Arab kids at our school. We all wore the same haircuts.

I even imagined that our mothers would get together. A kind of hair cutting convention where they talked about proper bowl sizes, shears and how much hair to trim around an ear to leave a landing zone for an airplane.

No matter how hard mom tried, the white sheet that she wrapped around my neck just couldn't keep those little snips of fine hair from dropping around my neck and under my shirt.

And boy, did they itch.

It didn't happen like that at the barber.

He used powder to brush it all off.

Mom just brushed my neck off, shooed me outside and carefully shook the sheet on the kitchen floor where she swept the cuttings into a neat little pile.

"Next," she'd yell smiling.

Dad would sit down dutifully.

Hey, back in the 60s, $3.50 for a hair cut, and a 50 cent tip, was a lot of money.

And mom saved us at least $11 a week.

For that, we got great food.

Mom couldn't really cut my hair the way I wanted, but she was one hell of a great cook.

What's In a Name?

Adlai Shalabi always had a hard time because of his name.
When he was growing up, he constantly had to fight to
get his teachers to pronounce his name correctly.
It was "Ad - Lee."
Simple. Straightforward. But Arab, nonetheless.
"I could never get the teachers to pronounce my name right,"
Adlai recalls.
"It was Adella. Udlay. Adelie. You name it, but it was never Ad-Lee."
This is a common problem that many Arabs experience.
Americans have a problem with our names.
I recall sitting in a political science class with Milton Rakove
when he came across the name of a student named Muhammad Zum
Zum.
Muhammad is the most common name given to a male child in
the world.
But as soon as Professor Rakove pronounced his last name, Zum
Zum, the professor started laughing uncontrollably.
It was wrong, and Rakove did not mean to intentionally
embarrass the student. But he did.
Muhammad was so angry and embarrassed by the apparent insult
that he stood up and started yelling at the teacher, in Arabic,
demanding that he apologize.
I recall that Rakove regained his composure and did apologize,
but the incident could not be erased from the minds of other
American students in the class, who saw Muhammad as the
distraction.
It was unintentional humiliation, but it was common.

No one at Joseph Warren Elementary school on Chicago's Southeast Side could pronounce my name correctly, either.

They always called me "Ha-NANE-yah," not "Han-na-NEE-ya," which is the correct Arabic pronunciation.

My gym teacher called me "Ha-NANE-yah." Other teachers called me "HAY-nee-ya."

Fortunately, my first name was very easy. Raymond.

For other Arabs, their names were Abdullah, Muhammed, Shukry, Fadi, Abdelaziz, Suheil or Assad.

Arab Americans found that other Americans simply refused to pronounce their names. It wasn't just that they were different, but also, we felt, because the names were "Arab."

So, most Americans ended up "assigning" nicknames to them. Muhammad was turned into "Mike." Fadi became "Fred." Assad became "Ass."

Many times, Arab Americans simply adopted American nicknames themselves, and offered them like a sacrifice to avoid the hassles some Americans have with Arab names.

But there was no nickname for Adlai Shalabi.

And nothing could have been more embarrassing than to have teachers at his elementary school constantly mispronounce his name.

Afterall, Adlai Shalabi attended Adlai E. Stevenson Elementary school on Chicago's Southwest side.

Muhammad Ali

This is the legend of Cassius Clay
the most beautiful fighter in the world today.
He talks a great deal, and brags indeed,
of a muscular punch that's incredible speed.
This brash young boxer is something to see,
and the heavyweight championship is his destiny.

Muhammad Ali, AKA Cassius Clay

There were two things in life that would draw my mother's ear to the radio back in the 60s and 70s.

The first was breaking news reports that followed the events of the Arab-Israeli wars.

But the one that brought the greatest joy was listening to the ringside announcer's calls of a Muhammad Ali fight.

As much as African Americans saw Muhammad Ali as the symbol of success over insurmountable odds and a nation of discrimination, he was also one of the earliest and greatest heros for Arab Americans, too.

He was our champion, the first American sports hero to change his name and adopt a Muslim name that was an Arab name too!

It didn't matter whether you were Christian or Muslim Arab. Muhammad Ali was the champion for us all.

We joined with African Americans in rallying behind him as he faced boxing contenders in the ring, responded defensively to attacks from the American public, and stood tall against the attacks from the US Government.

Many of his associates and aides, in fact, were Arab Americans.

Muhammad Ali was "our" celebrity who we shared with African Americans.

And we stood by him in solidarity when he converted from his Baptist religion to become an American Muslim, changing his name from Cassius Clay to Muhammad Ali in 1964.

The criticism, we felt, was partially directed against him because he was a Muslim.

It was at this point that we used the non-Arab, American logic that is unable to distinguish between Christian or Muslim Arabs.

Ali lived, for a time, near where I worked as a grocery bagboy for Jewel on 87th and Stoney Island.

I met him several times during the late 60s, a time when he was banned from boxing because of his refusal to be drafted and because of his criticism of the Vietnam War.

Ali would pull up in a light brown Lincoln Mark II and enter the store with several of his friends. Each time, he would look for my check out aisle so that I could carry his bags out to his car. I was probably the darkest person working at the Jewel back then, which consisted of a ruling class click of white employees and managers. In fact, you couldn't be promoted from bag boy to stock clerk, it seemed, unless you were white.

It was as if there were two society's at work, the white employees, and the rest. There was very little socializing between the two groups.

I managed to bridge that gap, making friends with the white employees, most of whom were Christian and middle class.

My supervisor let me in on the "secret," that they didn't hire Blacks and they didn't promote Jews. Sure enough, all of my Jewish friends remained as bag boys when I was promoted to the higher paying job of stock clerk, $3.75 an hour at union scale.

It was easy for Ali to pick me out in the store, my dark skin and dark black hair a sharp contrast to the other Jewel to the employees he might normally have seen. Maybe it was a sense of reverse discrimination. Or maybe it was just Muhammad Ali playing by the rules set by white society.

Ali always gave me a crisp dollar tip, which back in 1968 was quite a tip for carrying out a few bags of groceries.

Years later, Ali would appear at Arab American functions speaking out for the Arab cause, defending Palestinian rights and greeting a visiting Arab sheikh, who often came to provide sizable donations to local store-front mosques (Muslim churches) on South Ashland Avenue.

I saw Ali, then, simply as a celebrity.

But to my parents he was more.

They loved to hear his name spoken on the radio and the television.

He was the "greatest," and he was loved like a member of our family.

And every time reporters would call out to Ali as "Cassius Clay," refusing to acknowledge his Muslim name, my mom would yell at the television or at the radio, "His name is Muhammad Ali. Why don't they call him by his name?"

At one time, Ed Lassman, president of the World Boxing Association, tried to strip Ali of his title because of his Muslim beliefs and his refusal to box under his "Christian" name, Cassius Clay. Lassman criticized Ali saying that he was not the kind of role model children in America needed.

My parents thought otherwise, and they always believed that it was American Jewish bias and Lassman as a symbol of that anti-Arab sentiment that existed in the American Jewish community.

Lassman was just one of a string of powerful white Americans who tried to always push Muhammad Ali down. But, he would never heel.

Of course, it didn't help that the spiritual leader of the Nation of Islam, Elijah Muhammad, spoke like a racist himself, denouncing whites and challenging their perceived superiority.

All this came at a time in our country when white flight and racism were common day events. The truth was that during those times, African Americans *were* discriminated against in our society. They *were* denied jobs because of their race and color of their skin. They *were* pushed into overcrowded, poorer quality schools. White homeowners ran in ridiculous hysteria when an African American family would move into their neighborhoods.

And to most whites, non-European immigrants were all African American. Arabs. Indians. Orientals. The whiter your skin and the more you looked like the "majority," the more accepted you became.

Muhammad Ali was the only African American that I can recall who shopped at the Jewel on Stony Island Avenue.

The Golden Gloved wonder not only had style, he had charisma. He was our David in a Goliath World of antagonism, a small reprieve in a world where Arab Americans felt like outsiders.

Muhammad Ali forced the world to give him the respect he deserved.

Just repeating his name gave us a sense of special power.

When Ali won his fights, we felt like winners, too!

I Wonder if John Wayne Ever Ate Mensiff?

Mom had really scrubbed the windshield of the Dodge clean. It glistened.

She cooked all day. And when she was done, she packed the lawn chairs in the car trunk with the food.

After all, it wasn't everyday that mom and dad would take the kids to the Drive-in.

We were on our way to see John Wayne on the Big Screen.

It was 1959 and *Rio Bravo* was at the Drive-in.

You could smell the cooked grape leaves through the back seat, simmering in a large metal pot in the trunk of the car. The pot was wrapped in heavy towels to keep it hot as we drove past the Drive-In ticket booth.

Dad careened the car through the narrow, dusty lanes as mom navigated to the right parking spot.

"Over there. No, here. It's better there. We can see the screen from here, *habibi.*"

It was all in Arabic, of course. Mom never spoke English to my father. Only to the kids.

I knew what she was saying, I just couldn't say the words.

My brother John, sister Linda and I were excited. The Drive-in was unlike the confines of a movie theater where we couldn't jump around or make noise. At the Drive-in, where we had gone only once before, we could romp around freely and make all the noise we wanted.

In 1959, no one thought about crime at the Drive-in. No drugs. No fear of being molested, or being robbed. Drive-ins were a part of that slice of apple pie that my dad worked 40 hours a week to enjoy.

I was only six, back in 1959. But I knew that my parents really liked John Wayne. And over the years, they really learned to love him.

He was tough and very macho. And as far as my parents were concerned, he was one of the few movie stars who did not rise to Hollywood fame killing Arabs.

My parents hated movies that made the Arabs looked bad. And nearly every Hollywood movie about the Middle East, Israel or the Arabs made the Arabs look bad.

Imagine growing up as a young child, and watching movies that made people who were your father, brother or cousins appear to be brutal killers.

It was like that in nearly every movie

John Wayne was a natural hero, especially to my brother, who was 11, who was into Westerns, and who was named John too.

The aroma of the grape leaves in the trunk continued to fill the car.

Dad opened the door and we all stepped outside. You could hear the sound of the movie previews coming from hundreds of little boxes that hung by coiled wire from the parking polls.

Mom walked around to the back of the car and opened the trunk. Dad handed each of us an aluminum folding chair. We carried them to the front of the car and spread them out, facing the giant outdoor screen.

A lot of people brought lawn chairs to the Drive-in, back then. It wasn't that unusual.

But nobody ate like we did at the Drive-in.

Mom carried the large steel pot, covered with a flat metal top and tightly wrapped with towels as perfectly as any mother could fold a towel to secure the heat and flavor.

It was a precious cargo. While we could pull over almost anywhere to pick the leaves from the grapevines, we had to drive for miles to find a small store that sold the spices that made the meal Arabic.

I recall going to a small shop owned by a Mr. Ziyad. We had to drive more than an hour to get there. Mr. Ziyad was from a small town in Palestine called Yalo. Today, he is one of the largest distributors of Arabic foods and spices in the United States and you can buy his products at Jewel.

But back then, you could never get Arabic spices or ingredients at a regular American grocery store. You could only buy them at Arab stores.

Mom passed out the paper plates and she carefully lifted pieces of the wrapped grape leaves from the still warm pile in the pot.

The steam rose from the grape leaves inside, wetting our appetites.

Each grape leave is individually wrapped by hand. My mom's hands, to be exact. It took hours to prepare a full meal, maybe wrapping more than 200 leaves, carefully folding the sides into the center, and rolling the leave around a clump of rice and spiced ground lamb. The leaf tip neatly folded around until it formed a small, dark green cigar that was lifted from the kitchen table and carefully placed in its proper position on top of the lamb slices and the other grape leaves that had already been rolled.

Cooked slowly for several hours over a low flame, and sealed in the pot where they steamed to perfection, grape leaves are my favorite meal, but not the traditional meal of a "real" Arab.

That meal is called "*Mensiff.*"

Mensiff is a similar dish of rice topped with carefully cooked lamb chunks, served on a large, broad metal plate.

Mensiff is not supposed to be eaten with a fork or a spoon.

And although I had never seen my relatives eat their food with their hands any other time, eating mensiff with your hand was required. You poured the sauce on the rice, and then filled your palm with the rice, squeezing and tossing slightly, and then popping it into your mouth.

With your hands, you would tear off a chunk of freshly cooked lamb.

If cooked right, the lamb would fall off. You wouldn't have to tear.

Mensiff is truly an Arab dish, served in the homes, tents and gatherings of almost every Arab family in the Middle East.

And while mensiff and grape leaves both smelled equally good, you couldn't bring mensiff to the Drive-in. It was too messy to eat.

My hand was too small to eat *Mensiff*, anyway. Grape leaves were a more convenient meal to bring with you to the Drive-in.

Mensiff was for those times when the entire family got together for a holiday, like Easter, which always came one week after the rest of the world celebrated Easter. Ours was Orthodox.

I remember the family next to us at the Drive-in, two cars away -- no one would park any closer -- staring at us as we ate. Probably wondering what it was that smelled so good.

I'm sure if they were hungry, my mother would have offered them something to eat, too.

Arab meals were more than just meals, they were events.

My mom never made a meal that was "just enough" for the family.

It was always, too much.

And "too much" was perfect for Arab tradition of giving. We always made too much food because we expected to share it with others.

But even my mother, in this country only seven years by the time *Rio Bravo* had hit the Hollywood screen, must have known enough not to offer grape leaves to strangers at the drive in.

As I ate, I watched the people in the nearby car watching us, glad that mom had brought something "normal" like grape leaves, instead of something "strange" like *Mensiff*.

It would take courage to eat *Mensiff* in public, with your hands.

The kind of courage that John Wayne had.

The Hollywood Arab

Oh, I come from a land, from a faraway place;
Where the caravan camels roam.
Where they cut off your ear, if they don't like your face;
It's barbaric, but hey, it's home.

Original lyrics from the Disney movie *Aladdin*
before they were changed for video

Arab Americans who tried to advocate their "cause" never had a chance in this country.

First of all, we did not and still do not understand the concept of "perception."

And while Arab Americans are always angry with their portrayal by the media on TV, in Hollywood or in the news media, they see the media as a threat rather than as a potential instrument of salvation.

But those concepts are far beyond the challenges that faced my parents.

Most of the anti-Arab hatred that we encountered came not from neighbors, but from a little electronic box in our living room called the television set.

In the 50s, TV was a new concept.

But someone figured out early that it had a tremendous influence on the public.

As a child, I was glued to the children's programs and the cartoons.

How does your parent fight the influences of TV?

How could my mother or father counter the influences that

affected me through the television?

As an Arab American, these negative influences were great and difficult to counter.

Arabs were not just portrayed as villains, they were portrayed as sleazy, unsavory, and immoral.

The best known in this category was "Little Egypt," the woman who entertained at the Columbian Trade Exposition of 1892 in Chicago.

"Little Egypt" was the nickname of Fahreda Mahzar, the star performer in the Midway's Streets of Cairo exhibit. Ms. Mahzar danced what was then called the "Hootchie-Cootchie," a variation of a belly dance. Although Ms. Mahzar was originally from the Middle East, she was not Arab, but Armenian. (Many Armenians lived in Palestine among the Arabs during the Ottoman occupation. Most were Christians who fled Turkish/Muslim persecution.)

Her image was image, but very negative.

Nearly every villain in the early cartoons was a dark eyed, big nosed Arab. Unlike other stereotypes, the Arab stereotype was easier to identify. He always wore an Arab headdress and he had Arab names, like Hassan or Abdullah.

Ben and Ali were famous characters in a popular Christmas television special called *The Little Drummer Boy*. Written by Romeo Muller, narrated by Greer Garson, and highlighted by the Vienna Boys Choir. It was a family favorite.

Sure. The story about a little Jewish boy (who wears a yarmulke) who suffers at the hands of prejudice. Ben and Ali are Arabs with a protruding noses and large lower lips. One wears a scimitar in his belt. Ali wore an Egyptian Fez. He was an ugly and unsympathetic shyster always involved in some scam, including harassing the Jewish boy.

But if that were the only one.

These negative perceptions come from somewhere. They just don't happen.

One source for these stereotypes was the tension that exists between Arabs and Jews in this country caused by the Palestine conflict that dominated the greater part of the 20th Century.

Another source was simple bigotry and American policies that discriminated against Arabs as an unwanted alien. The discrimination that is taken for granted is the most dangerous.

Authors Jack Lait and Lee Mortimer wrote in their book *"Chicago: Confidential"* about several Arab restaurants in Chicago's "Arabic Quarter" at 18th and Michigan in the late 40s.

> *If you can digest such, there are several native restaurants serving Near Eastern delicacies which you are supposed to eat with your hands ... You will find no orgies out of the Arabian Nights here. Chicago's Arabs don't keep harems and if they did you wouldn't care to look twice at their women.*

Even before that, American immigration policy was to try and stop the influx of Arabs into this country.

Arguing that Arabs were not white, Richard Campbell, Chief of the US Naturalization Bureau officially fought the naturalization of "Syrians" and directed judges and US Government Attorneys General to reject citizenship petitions from Syrians.

Many Arabs crossed the Atlantic (an Arabic word which means *Sea of Darkness*) to come to the United States.

While the great mass influx did not begin until years later, the first official contact between American and Arab merchants occurred prior to the Civil War in 1857 when the Army purchased some 66 camels to help cross the deserts of New Mexico, Texas and Arizona. Hadji Ali, one of the trainers brought to this country with the camels, later became somewhat famous as one of the first officially recognized Arabs to settle in America. Better known as "Hi Jolly" because his name was so strange to the Americans, the Arizona Department of Highways erected a pyramid on "Hi Jolly's" grave, topped with a copper camel to memorialize his pioneering role in this country.

Not withstanding the fact that the US Army's intended use of a camel corp failed.

The first Arab immigrants came from Syria and Lebanon through Ellis Island around the 1870s.

Arabs were not even officially recognized as such by immigration officials until 1899 when they were separated from the "Turks in Asia" classification, almost 30 years later.

In many states, governments prohibited Arabs from voting, arguing that they fell under laws restricting the voting franchise by "Yellow" people. That law remained in force until 1915.

A few Arabs from North Africa settled in South Carolina in the 1790s, forcing local law enforcement officials to distinguish "the sundry Moors" from Africans, and protecting them from the special codes set aside for Black slaves.

It wasn't until Danny Thomas (Amos Jacobs) broke ground with TV's *Make Room for Daddy* that Americans were acquainted with the innocent antics of Uncle Tannous (Hans Conried). Eleven years in prime time and nine seasons in reruns proved its popularity.

But Uncle Tannous and Danny Thomas were so far removed from Arab American life that the show did little to soften the anti-Arab hysteria that dominates American TV and Hollywood movies.

We knew Uncle Tannous was Arab. But nobody really said that on TV.

The movie that Arabs hate the most is one of America's favorites, *Exodus*, the story of how the Jews settled Palestine. How they made the desert bloom, turned the rock-strewn Palestine into a lush fertile land.

An epic drama, *Exodus* stereotyped the profile of the only acceptable Arab, a Muslim leader who befriended the "Jews" who was later murdered by his own people, hung in the public square with a Jewish star carved with a knife into his chest.

Was that a warning, or were we supposed to be honored?

We were the bad guys.

All you had to do was look up the word "Arab" in an American dictionary or thesaurus: "sometimes offensive, urchin, gamin."

Arab Americans were especially sensitive to this.

We were engaged in our own, internal conflict.

Like many Arabs born in the United States, I was very ashamed of the people who claimed to be Arab leaders both in this country and abroad. Arab leaders who said they wanted to "liberate" Palestine obviously were doing nothing and were interested only in preserving their own power and possessions.

I was proud of my culture and Arab heritage, but I was caught between discrimination in this country and embarrassed by Arab political incompetence.

As leaders, they were inarticulate and unvisionary. They seemed to worship the empty word.

As a military force, the Arab armies were untrained, ill-equipped and poorly led. Their threat was greater than their action.

As a political entity, the Arab cause was portrayed in ridiculous, childlike terms poisoned by emotion and illogic.

Much of this feeling was reinforced by Hollywood movies that portrayed Arabs in the most derogatory and negative light.

In fact, of some 100 movies with an Arab or Middle East related theme, only one portrayed Arabs in a positive light. That movie was Disney's animated feature, Aladdin. The film included lyrics derogatory toward Arabs, that were lated changed after protests from the American Arab Anti-Discrimination Committee, when the film was released on video.

But, when the only positive movie about your ethnicity is an animated cartoon where the hero is a WASP-looking, small-nosed Arab -- he looks more European than Arab -- you have to wonder whether Hollywood is intentionally portraying Arabs in such a bigotted manner.

An Arab Bas Mitzvah

Whose side are you on, Herman?"

My friends stood around me, asking me the question over and over again?

"Whose side are you on?"

It was June 6, 1967 and we were standing outside of Joseph Warren Elementary school, the point on the map that brought together four culturally and ethnically different communities.

"Come on, Herman. Whose side?"

"Well," I said. "I'm not on anyone's side?"

How could I be?

Forget for a moment that all my friends were Jewish. And that while they knew I was "Arab" they also had embraced me as a friend and had nicknamed me "Herman" ... a personal induction into the world of Chicago's South Side Jewish Community.

The name, "Herman," was like a VIP pass into Jewish culture. The Henry Horn Jewish Community Center. The Hebrew School across the street. Mel Markon's Restaurant on the crest of Pill Hill. And, access to the world that dominated the school and the community.

Maybe they called me Herman because in Hebrew school and at the JCC, they were taught that the Arabs were their enemies, just as in my community, I was taught that the "Jews" were my enemy. I couldn't be an Arab to them, if I was an "Herman."

I was clearly as much a contradiction to them as they were to me. Yet, this was the only real level of contact between our two communities, at the grammar school level. Our parents never met. They never got together at social gatherings. Or, for that matter, in any environment where they were each recognized as Arabs or

Jews. They did meet as "parents," at the PTA meetings, although my parents rarely saw any other Arab parents at the meetings. And there was a healthy Arab American community in our neighborhood.

Set aside all of that, and I had to still ask "How could I be on anyone's side?"

In less than 24 hours, we were being told, Israel's "tiny, defenseless, ill-equipped" army had crushed the "greater, better equipped" armies of four Arab nations: Egypt, Jordan, Syria and Lebanon.

I didn't know that was a news media lie. It was just another media perception sold to the American public. I had only turned 14, by then.

How could I know that Israel's army was ranked number three in the world, even back then. And that the so-called Egyptian Army was a rabble of peasants led by political hacks who offered ancient and useless weapons and out-of-date systems and tanks?

Jordan's army still road camels and horses. Syria was even worse than Egypt. And Lebanon. That's a joke. Their army was the beginnings of a private militia, Cub Scouts with guns.

I didn't read anywhere in the news media that the Egyptian Army had never crossed the Sinai and had never "invaded" or set foot on Israeli territory when Israel launched a pre-emptive strike. Even today, the media is filled with descriptions of how the Arabs "attacked" Israel causing Israel to defend itself.

That idea of defending oneself is a very American concept, and Americans admired those who displayed American concepts.

Emotion, anger, cultural differences, language barriers and strange religions were things that Americans refused to admire or even understand.

The facts didn't mean anything when the world told everyone that Arab bluster had forced Israel's hand, the hand of a "tiny, innocent nation surrounded on all sides by 22 hostile Arab countries each with the most sophisticated and modern weaponry of our time.

Their backs to the sea."

And, there was Egypt President Gamal Abdul Nasser's infamous boast, that the Arabs would "drive the Jews into the sea."

He didn't say "Drive the Israelis into the sea."

He didn't say "Drive the Zionists into the sea."

He said "Drive the Jews into the sea."

And anything that had to do with criticizing "Jews" was considered, especially in this country, anti-Semitic.

Didn't Nasser know, I thought?

Wasn't he smart enough to realize that there was a way to defeat Israel, in the real battlefield of the news media?

I stood there circled by my friends, all Jewish, and all I could do was shrug my shoulders. Had Nasser given me anything to be proud about in this whole mess?

And in grammar school, the 8th grade home room teacher asked the class to pause for 15 minutes so that the Jewish students could pass around a canister with a picture of Nasser and ask for donations to support the Israelis, who were under attack.

In that environment, that intense social pressure, I found myself helping them to pass the canister around the class so they could collect money to fight my own people.

It was a humiliating experience, something that bothered me only years later.

Living between Pill Hill, Jeffery Manor, Calumet City and South Shore, in an area we called South Shore Valley, I grew up with middle class Jewish families.

Pill Hill is where all the rich people lived. Most were Jewish doctors and lawyers. In 1969, when white flight chased all the Jewish families up north to Niles and Skokie or further south to Olympia Fields, and the Christian families west to Oak Lawn and Burbank, Pill Hill became a center of wealthy, upperclass African Americans.

The Synagogue became a Baptist church. Mel Markons was shuttered and the JCC was abandoned for years.

But, before white flight, it was all an economic thing. My middle class Jewish friends didn't call the Jewish families in Pill Hill "rich Jews." We just called them "rich."

Joseph Warren was an eclectic mix of culture. There were clear divisions that no one ever taught us about in school, but that we saw easily as we walked from our homes to the classrooms. And, as long as the divisions remained intact and every ethnic group remained in their own area and didn't mix, everything was fine.

The Mexican and Puerto Rican students lived in Calumet, across the viaduct and toward the East. The Blacks lived north of 71st Street, toward South Shore, a neighborhood that was fighting white flight. The rich Christian families, Protestants, mostly, lived in Jeffery Manor, to the South, across 95th Street. The Jews and Arabs and other middle class Americans lived in South Shore Valley. The rich Jews lived in Pill Hill.

That's the way it was.

Nobody complained.

In school, the Jewish students were very educated and had the highest grades. They were active in sports, and all the extra-curricular activities that existed.

My friends styled and dried their hair every morning and their hair was perfectly combed across their foreheads. They went to the barber shop and got duck tails.

They wore Penny Loafers with pennies actually stuck inside the front band of the shoe. No socks, and sweaters with no shirts underneath.

The favorite shirt was a Gant. It had a "Lucky Loop" on the back under the neck line, that the girls collected.

If you didn't have one, you weren't cool.

Very casual. Very neat.

It wasn't until years later that I discovered the secret of a blow drier. My hair was always curly. I thought it was because I didn't go to the same barber as my friends, and because my mom cut my hair in the kitchen with a white sheet wrapped around my shoulders. The sheers cleaned my neck. The scissor evened my hair around the sides.

Mom loved to cut my hair. But it also saved a lot of money.

The Christian kids were mostly called "greasers." They slicked their hair back with VO 5.

They wore dark clothes, tight black pants and slick, black high heeled and pointed toed shoes.

They seemed to hate school and got poor grades. They liked to fight, and they were often portrayed as the bullies.

I would go back and forth between dressing for my Jewish friends and my non-Jewish friends. Occasionally, the lines would blur, but the reaction was always clear, as it was one day when I went to school wearing socks that were thin and typical of my greaser friends. They were off-color green with all kinds of colored patterns on them.

Robin, who sat in front of me, turned around and looked at my socks. She had a smile on her face when she exclaimed without hesitation, "Those socks are pathetic."

I smiled, thinking that "pathetic" was a compliment. They w ere the same kinds of socks that my dad wore, and that my cousins wore. And that even some of my greaser friends wore.

Eventually, I did look it up "pathetic" in the dictionary at home and never wore the socks again.

These were the stereotypes that I had to maneuver among.

The Arab kids were hidden in this landscape. We blended in, some with the Jewish kids, most with the greasers.

Some of the Arab kids hated Jews and refused to play with them in the playground.

It was literally like being in two societies. I was privileged to be accepted by both. Educating in one sense, confusing in another.

Those Arab kids that I knew who spoke better Arabic than English, had a better education on the facts of the Middle East and Palestine, which meant that they hated the Israelis, blamed the Jews and wouldn't hang around them if their lives depended on it.

Those like me who spoke English and only understood Arabic because that is all my mom spoke at home, lived in a dreamland that escaped all the hatred that was building between Arab and Jew.

Their paths rarely crossed, although I quickly recognized that the Jewish kids lived a better life, had the favor of the teachers and were more fun to hang around.

During the day, the educated kids controlled the schools.

But 45 minutes after school let out, the playground was controlled by the greasers.

It was sort of like a shift change.

We would leave, and the tough guys would come in.

No one from my crowd ever went back to school after it was closed.

After school, we went to the JCC. On Thursday nights, each week, the JCC would feature teen dances and socials. The Beatles and the Roiling Stones and the rock music revolution were a great influence on society and everyone responded to it differently.

The Jewish kids also formed fraternities in grammar school and also in high school.

I was allowed to hang around the Jewish fraternity, "The Mafia," at the JCC, but during high school, I was not allowed to join the Jewish fraternities there. Achates was the most popular fraternity. My friends never explained why I had been blackballed, and I never asked.

We stayed friends during our two years at Bowen High school, until white flight changed the world.

Where I could go, though, was to the Hebrew school.

I went there a lot with my friends as their guest. The Rabbi didn't mind. He was always very pleasant, dressed in a dark black robe wearing his yarmulke on his head. I even wore a yarmulke, too.

The school was cleaner than the grammar school and had more activity rooms.

It was fun. There were many things to do there. Hebrew school was full of activities.

That was during the week, in the evenings after regular school. Each Sunday, my parents also took me to the Arab school. My mom and dad always fought over whether or not I should speak Arabic. I was 14 and they were still arguing about whether I should learn another language.

Ironically, I had learned it. I could speak it, but never did. I learned it by listening to my mother, who spoke it all the time, and my father, who always responded in English.

Dad had really bought into the American dream bit. He was many years older than my mother, married in an arranged marriage after his first wife, a German American woman he had met while in the US Army, had died giving birth on Christmas Eve to my brother.

Maybe that would sour anyone about life. He was always such a contrast to my uncles, who always spoke Arabic. All my cousins spoke Arabic, too.

My mother would sneak me to Arabic school after church.

The room was always some empty, dirty hall with wood floors. Metal folding chairs were arranged in rows, and a teacher would stand at the front.

The teacher was not a nice guy, always yelling at everyone, always telling you that you were "*majnoon*," or crazy if you didn't answer the right way. Some of the kids were "*shitton*," the devil.

The other Arab kids in the class all seemed to be poor, too. They didn't wear Penny Loafers or Gant shirts. They looked like they bought the clothes from the same bargain basement that my mom often took me.

The discussions always took on a political side, and the teacher often talked about Israel, Zionism and Jews.

And everything else was about Islam, even though I was Christian.

It wasn't fun at all.

I went to church every Sunday. At first, the Baptist Church was the only church in the area that would accept my parents.

Later, when some Arab families got together and formed a Greek

Orthodox Church, the religion of my parents, we would go to that church. At first it was a small building. Later, they bought an old abandoned Catholic parish church with the steeples and old facade.

But, it took almost an hour to drive there.

Finally, my parents enrolled me at a Lutheran Church in our neighborhood where I received my confirmation.

My parents still went to their Orthodox Church. I went to the Lutheran Church. And occasionally, my mom would reminisce about the excitement of the Baptist Church on Stoney Island Avenue when we were young. "It was always so exciting," she would recall.

I never did tell my parents that the pastor always talked about the righteousness of Israel -- the biblical Israel, of course. But it always seemed like the pastor was talking about the present.

My Jewish friends always seemed to protect me from "myself."

They didn't like the way I dressed, so they gave me clothes after I left my house on the way to school.

I took my socks off and wore the Penny Loafers like they did. I even finally convinced my mom to buy me jeans.

But by the age of 13, my mom helped get me a job.

The Burger King down the street from our home was owned by another Palestinian.

Mom brought me to him and asked if he would hire me. He did, putting me to work, under aged, at 95 cents an hour placing meat patties on the Burger King broiler conveyer belt. Back then, Whoppers only cost 35 cents. McDonalds didn't exist and the concept of "fast food" was slowly endearing itself into the foundation of the American dream.

During the day, mom worked at the Solo Cup factory in Jeffery Manor. Dad walked six blocks from our house to the Jeffery Avenue bus and took that downtown to work at Sinclair Oil Company. Just before it came time for him to retire, they laid him off. He always said it was because he was an Arab and the bosses didn't like him.

I can never forget his image. Clean, iron-pressed white shirt, neatly tied dark tie, inexpensive, off-the-rack suit, and heavy camel hair coat, dad still could not fit in as an American.

It didn't matter that he served during World War II with the OSS in Europe and that he was discharged with Honors. It didn't matter that he tried to blend in, speaking perfect English, he was still an Arab. He never let the bitterness show.

I earned my own money at a very young age and went out and started to buy some of my own clothes.

At the Burger King, I started to see a whole new crowd of people. Greasers who would hang out there at night and smoke cigarettes. Girls who didn't reject me and thought I was cute. People who always spoke badly about my Jewish friends.

I never told them that I spent a lot of my time with Jews at their homes, at their parties and even at their Synagogues.

The Jewish religion was a religion filled with culture. It seemed different from the Christian religion which lived in the "now." The Jewish religion seemed to live in tradition.

And, in Jewish tradition, a Jewish boy becomes an adult at the age of 13. The Bar Mitzvah is the ceremony in which Jewish Boys are given the privilege of performing mitzvot -- the commandments in life.

I never knew this studying at the Lutheran Church, but there were more than just 10 commandments. There are, actually, 613.

I went to several Bar Mitzvahs, but was invited to only one Bas Mitzvah, the equivalent ceremony for young Jewish girls recognized by the Reformed Jewish church.

Laura, who I really liked, invited me to her Bas Mitzvah.

She lived in Pill Hill, and she was one of the only Jewish girls who would talk to me. The rest knew I was Arab and pretty much ignored me, except when they were insulting me.

My friends and I took criticism from them in the context of normal boy-girl relationships. We didn't like them. They didn't like us. I didn't realize that with me, it was a little more.

I'm Glad I Look Like a Terrorist

I wanted to go to Laura's Bas Mitzvah.

Saturday morning, I went to the Synagogue dressed in my cheap, grey suit, white shirt and thin dark tie. The tie was a clip-on tie that I got as a present from one of my uncles who owned a clip-on tie making factory in Baranquilla, Colombia.

I looked just like my dad. My Sunday shoes were polished. My hair was neatly combed back. But despite all my efforts, I could never look like my friends.

Their clothes were always perfect, fashionable, modern and expensive looking. Their hair was always so perfectly combed. In the age of the music revolution and the Beatles, appearance was everything.

Laura invited me to the party she had at her house in Pill Hill. I wanted to look special.

Mom took me to Goldblatts bargain basement where we rummaged through a table of sale shirts until we found one made by Gant.

It was a Gant with a Lucky Loop on the back, the style that everyone wore in school. But, of course, it had one slight problem. It was multi-colored, like a rainbow. Not exactly what my friends wore, but close enough, I thought.

I bought a pair of orange corduroy, hip-hugger bell bottom pants with a large buckled, brown leather belt.

And, I put on a grey checkered sports coat.

It was the only one I could afford.

I made my mom buy me Penny Loafers and wore them with no socks.

I thought I was cool. Just like my friends.

"Jesus Christ, Herman. What the hell is that?" Bruce blurted out when he saw me. We all met at his house before the Bas Mitzvah party.

"What do you mean?" I asked really surprised.

"You can't go like that?"

He never did explain what he meant.

But he gave me a thin, dark grey tie.

It didn't have the white plastic flaps or the center snap and I didn't know how to tie it.

He turned me around and helped me tie it, explaining that what he was doing was tying a Windsor Knot. There was a Full Windsor, and there was an Half Windsor, he explained. These were the knots of ties, he said.

Where'd he learn that?

Laura's house was very cool, so much different from my family's small two-story little Georgian on 89th and Luella Avenue. (George and Georgette Hanania lived in a Georgian and went to St. George Church. Hmmmm!)

Everything there was so beautiful.

Downstairs in a "family" room -- only the real rich had "family" rooms -- a band that Laura's parents had hired, played songs by Herman's Hermits. They sang all the songs we heard on the WLS Silver Dollar Survey.

I was really enjoying the music when I suddenly felt someone's hand grab my shoulder.

"What happened to you?" Laura's father asked me as the other parents stood around and watched.

I looked right at him and I never did understand what happened next.

My mouth took over from my brain and the words just spilled out like marbles from a bag.

Laura stood next to him as I spoke ... "Well, I ... I ... I ... was on my way home from the Syn ... Syn ... Synagogue after the se ... se ... service ... and, ah ... ah ... a car drove by and splashed m ... m ... mud on my shirt and suit from the curb ... and, ah ... I w ... w ... went home and had to change ... and, ah, my m ... m ... mom wasn't home ... and, ah, I didn't know what to wear because everything was dirty ... and, ah, hadn't been cleaned ... and, ah, I didn't know what to ...." I was a babbling fool.

If I only had this kind of imagination in English class, I might have gotten good grades. (My grades were so bad, I recall a teacher telling my mother once that if I really tried hard, I could be a C student someday.)

Laura's father smiled. It wasn't a mean smile. It was a nice smile. A sympathetic smile. Like he knew.

"Don't worry. It's okay. Let me help you."

He helped me take off the gray plaid jacket and he put it on a rack near the door far enough away so that everyone else's eyes would be safe.

He untied the tie and put it in the jacket pocket. He unbuttoned my collar.   "Now, go and enjoy yourself."

I was sweating like crazy, thankful that, at least, I didn't wear a clip-on tie.

"That was a Full Windsor Knot," I told Laura's father proudly. "There's a Half Windsor Knot, too!"

This Won't Hurt a Bit

Bill and I were always in competition.

He was my best friend.

We differed on almost everything, from class room studies to politics. I liked to study. He didn't.

But that didn't mean that Bill wasn't up on current events.

In fact, Bill was an enthusiastic supporter of George McGovern. I liked Richard Nixon. Bill knew the reasons why he liked McGovern. For my part, dad was a Republican and I guess I was too!

We used to have arguments forever about Nixon and McGovern, like anyone really cared about what we thought.

We both played guitar. And while I had an affection for science and biology, Bill loved cars.

He knew more about my Chevy SuperSport than I did, and all the improvements we made to the car were his doing.

But before my dad bought me the SuperSport, my brother Johnnie sold me his Corvair, a cute little sports car that served well as my very first car. (I never did pay him the $300 I owed him for the car and, frankly, I don't think he ever expected to be paid. But he did expect to use it when he came back from college on the weekends.)

The Corvair had one major problem. A tie-rod on the right side was loose, and it eventually broke.

So, to steer the car, I had to tightly hold the steering wheel in place. If I let go, the tie-rod on the left side would pull the wheels to the left, forcefully.

So, I just didn't let go.

Bill and I and another friend, Injun, drove everywhere. It was our

I'm Glad I Look Like a Terrorist

first car.

Mom and dad paid the insurance, I thought. Bill, Injun and I paid the gasoline.

Everything was going fine until one day, Bill and I got into one of our arguments about Nixon and McGovern.

We went back and forth, Bill concerned that Nixon would get elected and the world would be screwed. He could never explain why, but he insisted he knew better.

Injun simply didn't care. Injun was more than 6 feet tall, lean and mean. And whenever we got into a fight that Bill couldn't handle, Injun cleaned up.

They knew I was a wimp and couldn't fight. But I was smart and could get us out of jams.

We were driving around in Burbank when Bill and I went at it. Yelling back and forth about Nixon and McGovern, pushing and shoving, blowing smoke in each other's faces. We both smoked Winstons, although I had smoked filterless Camels for a number of years.

It was macho to smoke when you were 16. The ads were everywhere. No tough guy didn't smoke.

Anyway, suddenly our argument turned to grades.

Mine were poor, but they were better than Bill's. I don't even know if Injun was still in school or not. He was sitting in the back seat, anyway, while Bill and I wailed.

And that's when the subject turned to science.

"Hey, Bill. You think you're so smart?"

"Yea."

"Can you dissect a frog?"

Bill's jaw dropped. What the hell was I talking about?

"A frog. Can you dissect a frog and name every part of its internal anatomy?"

That showed him, I figured.

Bill started laughing.

"A Frog?" You f-in idiot. A Frog?"

Obviously, Bill had no respect for my prowess in the Biology lab.

As we started shoving each other, the lit end of my Winston broke free from the cigarette and landed on my shirt. The hot embers smoldered away through the material until it burned my chest and I let out a howl.

Removing both hands from the steering wheel, I started to brush my chest to stop the pain.

Bill was yelling "Dissect a frog?" over and over again as the car careened sharply to the right. Over the curb, skidding off the side of an Oak Tree, and crashing into the steep cement steps of this beautiful home.

My face slammed against the dash. Bill's head was bruised -- punishment for challenging my scientific skills -- and Injun was yelling, "The cops have a warrant out for me. I can't be here."

Injun jumped out of the car and Bill followed behind.

As they took off down the street, I could feel warm liquid -- my blood -- oozing from my nose, covering up the burn mark in my shirt.

I remember sitting at the police station holding my face up, trying to stop the bleeding and watching as everyone grimaced as they looked at me and walked by.

I turned to a mirror and saw that my nose was literally push sideways over my left cheek and under my left eye.

It was too numb to hurt, but it sure scared the hell out of me.

While Arabs and Jews have so many differences, one thing we share is an affection for nose doctors. Rhinoplasties run in nearly every Arab and Jewish family.

We had our share.

Of course, only the women had their noses done.

It was okay for a man to have a big schnoz. Jimmy Durante was always a favorite in the Hanania household at night.

So it was easy to find a doctor to fix my nose, that sat resting nicely under my left eye, covered with thick white gauze and white surgical tape.

The Burbank Police felt sorry for me and couldn't let me out into the world looking too much like Quasimodo.

Mom called "Uncle" Nadim, a surgeon at Northwest Memorial Hospital downtown.

He did her nose. He could fix mine.

Nadim was a great guy. Not really my uncle, he was the nephew of my Uncle Nick, who wasn't an uncle either.

That's how Arabs address each other, like family. Everyone is an Uncle or a "cousin" (*Khiya*, in Arabic.) "*Khiya* this. *Khiya* that!"

The way I looked at it, I was related to Gamal Abdul Nasser too and Yasir Arafat.

Nadim brought me into a surgical room filled with moveable lights, an examining table and surgical tools.

He assured me, everything was going to be fine.

He explained that it would be very easy to reset my nose, whatever that meant, and make it look good.

Mom was excited about Nadim fixing my nose, obviously hoping that the experience at the hospital would some how further encourage me to be a doctor.

"Be a doctor like your Uncle Nadim. Our your Uncle Nasri, or your cousin Daoud," mom would encourage. Daoud Hanania was in fact *the* chief surgeon in Jordan and was the doctor to King Hussein.

Examples of doctors were everywhere in our family, extended or otherwise.

Nadim called in a few nurses, then a few interns. And pretty soon, Nadim was giving a lecture, not to me, but to the new medical staff audience on how to set a nose.

The way I figured it, mom didn't pay Nadim, so Nadim was just getting something out of it by using me as a medical prop.

That's how Arab families are. Everything in life was free when it involved a relative, which explains why we called everybody "Khiya."

Anyway, I was laying on the table when I heard Nadim tell the growing crowd where to give the injections.

"Shots?" I asked. Nadim softly pushed my head back down.

"Won't hurt at all," he said.

Two in each nostril, two on top of the nose, or what there was of a nose.

And then we waited as he explained in medical terminology how he was going to move my nose from under my left eye to back in place, somewhat centered on my face.

(It was crooked to begin with.)

Not understanding all the medical jargon, I had no idea what he was saying.

That's when he put the sticks in each nostril, cupped my nose with one hand and slammed his other hand against my face, to re-break my nose.

My yell could be heard in the emergency waiting room four floors below.

He then used the sticks to lift my nose up and away from my face, and maneuvered it over where it rested for some 16 years, undisturbed by my political discussions and debates.

Using his palm, he precisely slammed it back down.

"There. Good as new."

Everyone was smiling, craning their necks to see my face.

Tears poured from both my eyes.

I'm Glad I Look Like a Terrorist

Under the Brookfield Zoo Lions

There isn't an open field of grass that can't be turned into a picnic site by an Arab family.

That's one thing about America that my dad and mom always loved. So many nice places to have a family barbecue.

We will spread our blankets and start dipping into our hummos anywhere where the sun shines and the grass rambles.

Brookfield Zoo and Grant Park are the two areas where our families most often held their picnics.

And, it didn't have to be a holiday either.

If you have to throw out the spare tire from the trunk to make room for the barbecue grill, so be it.

It was in Allah's hands!

My Uncle Khamis was the king of these outings. The unofficial picnic planner.

Uncle Khamis was a short, rotund person. Good natured, Khamis and Uncle Farid used to own and operate a women's lingerie store on West Lake Street in Chicago.

That was in the 50s and 60s when West Lake Street was still, somewhat safe.

Arab merchants often opened stores in African American communities.

The reason was simple.

White customers seemed to hate Arabs more. Black customers didn't seem to care. An Arab could open a store in a Black area easier than he could in a white area. And, we could also get a better bargain from the Jewish store owner who sold their inventories to us as we moved in and they moved out.

Most of the Jewish owned grocery stores in the inner city were sold either to Arabs or Koreans over the years.

There was also another even simpler explanation for why there were so many Arab owned stores in the back community: no one else wanted to go there. We saw it as opportunity.

My dad had five brothers. Two had died before I was born, the other three lived right here in Chicago. Uncle Edward was rarely around, seemingly the most injured by anti-Arab discrimination. He changed his name to Edward Johns -- John or Hanna was his father's name, and every Hanania son's middle name was John.

They were always close, and every chance they had, they would get together.

Khamis -- his name in Arabic means Sunday -- was unofficially in charge of bringing the Hanania clan together.

He planned the picnics. He supervised the cooking. He made sure everyone was contacted.

At Brookfield Zoo, under the stone Lions. At Grant Park. In the suburban forest preserves. Wherever we could lay a blanket.

Eight families, including cousins and other uncles, wives and children, gathered together in what must have looked like a once-in-a-lifetime family reunion.

We did it a couple times every year.

We always had to drive to a picnic.

And even after Uncle Khamis had completed all the preparations, all the brothers had to pick it apart.

There would be hours of discussions between the brothers about where we were going to go? How were we going to get there? Who was driving? And who would drive first?

This debate raged on even when we left and arrived at the designated picnic site in a caravan of five different cars.

Most of the time, we would arrive at the destination with little complications.

But boy did we ever dread getting lost.

How many times would this caravan pull over on the side of the road so the brothers could get out and examine the map?

Sometimes, they even got out of the car so that one of the sisters could use the bathroom on the side of the road in an emergency. The brothers would hold up a blanket.

It was rare, but it happens.

Aunt Ellen and her husband Uncle Joe would ride with us. Joe was Muslim from the Shalaby family. Ellen was my dad's sister. I was told that when they were married, there was a big family commotion, on his side and ours.

Arabs always talk about how close Muslims and Christians are, but when it came to your sister, look out.

"You can't trust those Muslims," an uncle would warn, setting Joe off with a response. "On Saturday it's the Jews and on Sunday it's us," they'd continue, mocking the Muslims with the fear that once Israel was "driven" into the sea -- their Sabbath is Saturday -- the Muslims would take care of the Christians in Palestine on Sunday, our Sabbath.

But these religious discussions were always overshadowed by the political discussions involving 1920 Palestine.

"We owned all the land," Uncle Khamis would begin. "The Jews stole it all away from us."

Dad would jump in at about that point because, like me, he figured the biggest problem Palestinians faced was not the Jews, but our own leaders.

"They stabbed us in the back. These big Arab families took all the land and sold them to the Jews, and then they told us that we lost Palestine after a brave fight in 1948. Garbage!" Dad would yell back.

Farid, Joe, Khamis, dad, and the elder sons would all fight to get a word in edgewise.

The debates always went from polite argument to yelling in a matter of minutes. Literally yelling.

It is not an Arab tradition to tolerate someone else's views. You made your point stronger by interjecting it on the other person as quickly as possible, and as loudly as possible.

The more emotion you put into the argument, the more right you were.

That seemed to be a trait not just of my uncles, but of almost every Arab who ever represented the Palestine cause on a TV or radio debate.

Arabic is a language that is spoken like a song. It is rhythmic. It is poetic. Poetry and song require emotion.

In later years, holding various positions in the Arab community, I always tried to force the people to debate the issues in English, figuring that the more they argued in Arabic, the more emotional the debate became. Because English was so hard for everyone, fighting in English toned the emotions and the arguments down.

All of the Uncles named their first born sons after their father.

There was no argument about that.

And every other kid took the middle name of the father.

My older brother was John George: John (Hanna) after my grandfather whom neither of us ever met, and George after our dad. Even my sister Linda's middle name was George, too, although she quickly changed it to Mary.

My eldest cousin's name was John Khamis Hanania.

And on and on through the entire family.

Actually, it was a slick way to create an easy to find genealogy.

My dad was George Hanna Hanania. His father was Hanna Mousa (Moses). Dad's eldest brother was Mousa Hanna Hanania, named after our great grand father.

You could follow the Hanania family back through history just knowing the names of the eldest sons, which automatically identified the father and the grandfather.

These and other things formed the basis for the discussions that took place while the women slaved over the picnic site itself, laying out the blankets, preparing the hamburger patties and the chicken.

They chopped up the salad and mixed them in the bowl.

They'd lay out the plates, cups and knives and forks.

We'd be jumping all over the Zoo grounds, running from cage to cage.

And our romps were not without their mishaps, either.

Linda and I stood next to the monkey cage, one day, when a monkey decided to relive himself (herself) right on top of us.

Another time, I recall climbing atop one of the stone lions at the Brookfield Zoo. Losing my balance, I tumbled to the pavement below, spraining my arm.

But back then, you didn't think about calling a lawyer.

I laid on the couch afterwards at Uncle Joe's house watching TV's *Family Classic's* presentation of *Moby Dick*.

Just the name Captain Ahab always set the uncles off too.

They hated anything that portrayed the Arabs badly.

Lawn chairs would be sprawled all over.

Arabs enjoyed being with their families. There was no shame in togetherness. It didn't matter how we looked to others. We were together. That's all that counted.

In later years, the picnics moved to the far west suburbs.

And eventually, they ended up in Uncle Khamis' backyard.

As the uncles died, the number of families attending the picnics seemed to dwindle.

The kids just didn't seem to carry on the same kind of tradition.

Most of us married American wives ... some of us more than once.

But the more Americans we brought into the family circle, the less the enthusiasm there was for a big family picnic.

"To the Arab from the Jew"

Even though my awakening as an Arab-American never really occurred until late in life, it was clear to me that being Arab American was like living two different lives.

The home environment was steep in Arab culture, tradition and food. My mother spoke Arabic to me and I would understand.

We would go to the Arab Church or visit relatives or other Arab families and the essence of the Arab experience was all around us, an aroma that was as heavy as the smell of spice.

It was only a short step from that environment to the American world where being an Arab didn't mean anything, and where the Arab identity was a foreign image rarely encountered.

Going to school was a good example. Although the school often celebrated the ethnicity of African Americans or the religion of the Jewish community, or recognized various ethnic holidays, nothing stood out that allowed me to hang my Arab American hat.

It was almost as if we didn't exist.

I left the house and closed the door on my Arab culture, and became an American with no identity. That's what it was like going to college, too.

Like all my friends in Bowen High school, nestled between the riches of Pill Hill and the poverty of Calumet, I applied to several colleges. I was accepted at Northern Illinois University.

The discussion about education in my home was never bothered by SAT and ACT scores, or a detailed scrutiny of my high school grades. They just were not very good.

It was always, "Ray, it's important that you go to college."

"Sure," I would say, unsure why I had to go.

I figured it was the only way I would get a job. And I certainly knew that I wanted to make more money than my father, who left the house at 6 am every morning to catch a bus to take him downtown. He didn't arrive home until late in the evening, usually around 6:30 pm. We didn't make much money. I could tell because I couldn't buy the same clothes that my friends wore and I never ran into them at Goldblatt's bargain basement, where my entire high school wardrobe originated.

I knew that I had to go to college in order to make the kind of money I wanted to live like my friends.

They had big homes. Ours was small and humble. Clean, of course. Every Christian Arab home was immaculate.

And, I wanted a big home.

That's what college represented to me when enrolled at NIU, which was located at DeKalb, Illinois, a cornfield town about a two hour drive from Chicago.

My grades were poor, in school, but I was accepted. And I was invited to a summer orientation where I met one of my closest friends, Stuart Rosenberg.

Stuart and I hit it off the minute we met sitting in the lobby of the Grant Towers North school dormitory.

We decided that day, after meeting dozens of very beautiful and encouraging girls, that we were going to drive together to Ft. Lauderdale, Florida.

After we got to know each other, and later learned that he was Jewish and I was Palestinian Arab, Stuart said that his parents seemed concerned about him driving alone to Florida with an Arab.

It wasn't racism at all. In fact, it was no different than what my mother said to me as I packed for the trip.

"He's Jewish?"

"Yea, mom. So?"

"Well, Jews and Arabs don't get along."

This was in 1970. Rock and Roll music was turning psychedelic and the world was certain that Arabs and Jews in the Middle East would never compromise. The Bible forewarned of Armageddon, and somehow the Arabs were responsible for that, too.

"Well, you just have to be careful," my mom said.

Frankly, I knew Stuart and he had the same kind of sense of humor that I had. I think it also helped that Stuart did not grow up in a predominantly Jewish neighborhood, and his girlfriend at that time was not Jewish either.

We both decided that if we were going to meet women, we would have to join a fraternity.

I knew fraternities were fun. My Jewish friends at Bowen High school were members of a private fraternity called Achates during their sophomore year. They partied every weekend and boasted about the sexual fun they had with girls.

Sexual fun with girls did not come for me until my senior year at Reavis High school, where I transferred when my parents moved to the Southwest suburbs. Most of my Jewish friends had moved North to Niles and Skokie, some far southwest to Olympia Fields.

We moved to Burbank, a middle class suburban hamlet with small frame homes and large back yards.

It was the last time I was to have Jewish friends until college. The few that lived in Burbank seemed to have a whole different approach to making friends with Arabs.

Stuart and I attended the College Fraternity Rush at a dozen fraternities houses.

Four of them ushered me out, saying they didn't want "niggers" or "spics" in their fraternity.

"You should be at Kappa Alpha Psi," one fraternity Rush chairman warned me as I left the frat house.

Stuart seemed to get encouragement, but left the houses that pushed me out.

Late in the evening, we finally stopped by the Theta Chi fraternity house where a party had raged on unrelentingly for more than two days.

Most of the fraternity brothers were drunk.

So when I filled out the application, they seemed very interested.

As it turned out, Theta Chi was having problems. With dropping pledge classes each year, they had to rush a minimum number of pledges if they planned to remain active. And what that all came down to was that if you planned to move out of the dormitory, if you were not rich, the cheapest alternative was to move into a Frat House.

Theta Chi had a great Frat House, but a lot of empty rooms.

They needed me, Arab or not.

Pledges are not invited to the meeting when the brothers decide who to enroll and who to reject.

The fraternity did what every other fraternity did, they gathered their members in the secret Frat Room, and passed around a box with white and black marbles.

Each member selected a marble and dropped it in the box as a picture of the prospective pledge was displayed on a screen from a slide projector.

They had to pass the box around six times when they came to me, because each time I was blackballed.

It only took one or two blackballs to keep a prospective student from becoming a pledge.

The crop was slim, like Nebraska during the dustbowl days at Theta Chi fraternity, that year.

I think we started out with 12 pledges. Out of that, they figured, only eight would remain after they spent our entire freshman year humiliating us.

Stuart was accepted immediately.

Had I not gone their with a friend, I would never have joined a fraternity.

I remember one of my Arab friends on campus, who I met at an Arab dinner there that my mother had attended, telling me that the fraternity system was "anti-Arab" at Northern Illinois and that I should quit.

I told him that no, the reason there are no Arabs in the fraternity system is that no Arabs tried to join.

It was an early lesson in the problems that my community faced in the United States.

Were we intentionally shut out of institutions or did we simply not try to get in?

That lesson struck home hard as I switched from a pre-med and biology major to a study of politics and journalism.

Why weren't there more Arabs in politics, or writing for the local newspaper?

Because we didn't file for candidacy? Or run for office?

I know there was a feeling that we were not wanted. Who wants to enter any arena where you are discouraged from participating. It's always better to go where you are invited, and avoid the places where your presence might turn sour.

Had I really followed that practice, I wouldn't have joined the fraternity, wouldn't have become a reporter and wouldn't have managed election campaigns in later years, all areas where traditionally, Arabs were excluded.

Because I quickly discovered that once the rest of the fraternity brothers got to know me, they respected me for my leadership and wit.

Of course, they also felt that molasses really looked good on a naked Arab's head standing in the middle of some farmer's cornfield.

"I bet none of these God damned farmers ever met an Arab that was ever as sweet as Ahab," one of the fraternity brothers yelled, as they left me in a cornfield five miles from the campus, wearing a towel and holding two dollars in change.

"Make sure to wear the towel around your ass, and not around your head!"

I used it to wipe as much of the molasses out of my hair and off my shoulders as I could. The molasses actually helped keep the towel around my waist.

I was damn cold walking down the farm road, hoping that a sympathetic, non-homosexual farmer would give me a ride back to the campus.

The night of our pledge initiation into the fraternity was memorable.

Blindfolded, we were led into a dark chamber where we recited the sacred Fraternity Pledge, and our pledge fathers instructed us on the secret handshake, secret passwords and secret history of Theta Chi.

My pledge father was Jewish, assigned to me on the first day of the four month pledge season during my freshman year.

Each pledge father had to hand carve a "paddle" that was embossed with the Theta Chi fraternity emblem, motto and names of the pledge and pledge father. I made one for him, hand carved and inscribed affectionately.

His read, simply: "To the Arab from the Jew."

It was quite a moment when I was inducted.

"The first Arab ever in Theta Chi," they yelled as we chanted "Theta Chi. Theta Chi."

Of course, it wasn't long ago that they were chanting "the first Jews" in Theta Chi either.

Stuart was assigned to a Jewish pledge father in the fraternity.

There were only a few.

A Media Consciousness

Arab mothers don't hope to see their children become journalists. A journalist, in Arab World perception, is in fact a propagandist for abusive political regimes and brutal government policies.

The Arab media, for the most part, is a media of acquiescence and obedience, a forum for special interest advocates. It is not a media of freedom nor is it a medium of free expression.

Arab World journalism is not the same as Western journalism at all, but a collection of opinions disguised as news. Arab journalism is mostly advocacy journalism.

This trait has carried itself intact from the Middle East to the United States in the cultural baggage of Arab , reinforced by years of anti-Arab biases in the American media.

The early Arab American media was, for the most part, a media of complicity and advocacy. The freedom of expression that existed, existed within narrow boundaries of community acceptability. The reporters who wrote or broadcast their stories usually were educated not in the standards of journalism but in the classrooms of political activism.

I recognized this as a problem for my community. And that motivated me to become a writer myself.

I was a pre-med major at Northern Illinois University who was quickly sucked into the culture of Arab student radicalism, demonstrations and protests.

While other students organized what I considered "positive" events such as celebrations and commemorations, Arab students organized protests against the actions of the others, specifically the Israeli students. "They" celebrated, we "suffered."

I quickly changed my major to politics, and found myself engaged in a no-win public debate, arguing the Arab cause. Because I was somewhat of an anomaly myself in my own community -- one of the few Arabs in this country whose immigrant father discouraged me from speaking Arabic -- my skills in writing and public debate were better than most of my peers. I satisfied American perception.

I didn't have an accent. I looked more "American" than most other Arab students or community leaders who were activists at the time.

I was elected the spokesman for the Arab-American Congress for Palestine, a Chicago area political organization that was heavily scrutinized by the FBI and the Justice Department, not for advocating terrorism, but for our activities in criticizing the policies of a foreign country, Israel.

That same year, I found myself on national television debating Middle East politics with the champion of Israeli eloquence, Foreign Minister Abba Eban.

I wrote dozens of Letters to the Editor to the major newspapers and the national magazines, and was published in most. For my community, my letters appearing in *Time* or *Newsweek* magazines were considered a major achievement.

While the route to Arab American leadership was effortless, it was a longer struggle upwards in journalism.

I had flunked English Composition 101 repeatedly. But I was fortunate that I had a high school teacher who saw a proficiency in me that few others recognized. Mrs. Harris asked me one day what my favorite hobby was. I told her it was music and playing the guitar. She asked me to write a column for the high school newspaper on rock music during my junior year.

In my senior year, I was named the Editor-in-Chief of *The Blueprint* Newspaper at Reavis High school in Burbank, Illinois, a suburb of Chicago.

My mother still wanted me to be a doctor, and when I graduated from high school, my brief career in journalism faded quickly as I pursued a pre-med major.

At Northern Illinois University, I was the first Arab student to be accepted into a campus fraternity, Theta Chi. As a joke, my Fraternity sponsor assigned to guide my pledge was Jewish. And when I completed by Fraternity Rush, I was presented with a Theta Chi paddle that read "To the Arab from the Jew."

Arabs were routinely blackballed from the fraternity structure.

Within months of my induction, I became the social chairman, an achievement I consciously sought to overcome the feeling of rejection that I encountered at the school. It also was an expression of my inner desire to communicate.

It cost me my grades, and by the end of my sophomore year, I had dropped out of school, and was ushered quickly to the offices of the local Air Force recruiter, running from a very vulnerable Vietnam War draft number of 65. I joined the Air Force just in time to observe the Yom Kippur, Arab-Israeli war in October 1973.

I found that there were a number of Arabs in the Air Force. We were constantly called "sand niggers" by our senior officers. But unlike African Americans in the service, we were not recognized as a legitimate ethnic group and there were no programs to deal with our problems. We down played our ethnicities in order to hide from the persecution and harassment, and the ridicule that followed the 1973 Arab Israeli War.

Most Americans saw the 1973 War not as an Arab victory, but as another Arab disaster saved only by the intervention of a manipulative Nixon administration.

But, in the minds of the Arab World, and Arab Americans, the 1973 War was a "victory."

In reality, the armies of Syria and Egypt were routed by the Israelis, not as quickly as they were in the humiliating defeat of the Six Day War in 1967, but just as publicly. Had the United States not stepped in to stop the Israelis, they would have occupied every Arab city from Cairo to Damascus.

My education as an Arab began in this wake of humiliation. We wanted so badly to experience the feeling of victory and success. We wanted so badly to restore our pride from the humiliation of the 1967 war, and the 1956 war and the 1948 war. We wanted so badly to restore our public image because shame is not a virtue in the Arab World.

Arabs do not suffer humiliation with grace.

I quickly recognized more than many others in my own community, that the real war was the war that we were losing in the American media. It didn't matter that we had done what everyone said we couldn't do -- surprise the Israeli army and recapture our lands -- because the media still portrayed it for what it really was: we won a battle but nearly lost the war. The media constantly harped on that fact, while Arab leaders insisted that we had won.

I realized that regardless of the reality of the 1973 war, or what we thought as Arabs, there was a "greater reality" that obscured the truth, and that was framed by the media. I realized that the media reinforced one perception over another, that the Arab armies had still failed to route Israel.

How we were portrayed in the media is important to us as a community. Because there was a thought formula, a media truism, that applied to us: the Arab armies had failed to defeat Israel, therefore, the Arab cause was an unjust cause against the righteousness of the cause of Israel.

Americans want simple answers. The American media gave them simple explanations through this greater reality.

I needed to become involved in journalism. I took it for granted in high school, ignored it in college, recognized how important it was during my service in the military and during the 1973 Arab-Israeli War, and made a decision to master it.

In 1975, I started an English language newspaper called *The Middle Eastern Voice*.

Nearly every major American printing house in the Chicago area refused to publish it. In fact, the only printer who would produce *The Middle Eastern Voice* was the Black Muslim Newspaper, *Muhammad Speaks* (later called *The Bilalian News*).

Ironically, the same printers who refused to publish my English language newspaper published other Arabic language newspapers. Why? Mainly because they could not read what was being published in those Arabic language newspapers. They could read *The Middle Eastern Voice*, though.

Few American stores would allow me to distribute *The Middle Eastern Voice* on their counters.

A west suburban newspaper publisher who refused to print *The Middle Eastern Voice*, called it "anti-Semitic." He had never even read any of the camera-ready copy.

A pharmacy near where I lived and where a significant Arab population was nurturing, said that I had to remove copies of the newspaper from their store because one "Jewish customer complained" that the newspaper was "anti-Semitic."

I told the owner it was not anti-Semitic, and said hundreds of Arab customers who lived near the store wanted it. But the owner insisted that the views of the one customer were more important, not because the customer was Jewish but because he, the owner, did not want any complaints.

But even many Arab stores refused to distribute it, some complaining because it carried an advertisement for an Arab Restaurant that included a picture of a belly dancer. Other Arab store owners were angry because it included a variety of views, rather than the one they supported.

This is a symptom of our problems with the news media, here and back home. The media of the Arab World did not tolerate freedom of expression, and therefore, as Arabs living there, we did not tolerate freedom of expression either.

Some Muslims in the Arab community accused the newspaper of being anti-Islamic for a variety of reasons including that I was Christian and a political "moderate;" a combination that is fatal in my community and would come back to haunt me later.

Although Muslim and Christian Arabs share a common destiny, they also share a thin line of distrust. There is an old Christian saying, somewhat racist and cruel, that contends, "On Saturday the Jews. On Sunday the Christians." It refers to the Sabbaths of the Jews and Christians and the fear that the Muslim world would swallow up the Christian identity, once they were done with the Jews, even though we were all "children of the Book."

I realized later that was in fact part of a larger problem in the Arab American community. We knew how to complain, but we didn't know when to complain.

Constantly being portrayed negatively by the news media injured us and caused many in my community to turn their frustrations against their own people. We become more critical of our own, because it is easier.

I know that if we were fortunate to have an Arab American woman win the Miss Universe Contest, instead of applauding her, many Arabs would criticize her for wearing a swim suit.

An Arab woman friend of mine -- a concept that is still very difficult to deal with as an Arab male in my society -- commented after the first Palestinian delegation had participated in the Olympics in Atlanta in 1996, that she dreamed of winning a Gold Medal in the swimming competition, but feared that she, too, would be criticized instead of applauded because she had to wear a swim suit.

Social and cultural taboos in the Arab World that had relevance in the 19th Century, are impediments to our Arab psyches and they temper our self-respect and pride.

In this same way, we are harmed by the American news media.

Most Arab Americans believe the American media is prejudiced against us, and controlled by the Jewish community which is engaged in a never ending struggle with the Arab community.

That's easier to accept than the difficulties of understanding the reality. It becomes a convenient excuse.

It's not that the American media opposes portraying Arabs in a positive light. That's too simple. Yes, some news editors fear criticism from the Jewish community. The reality is more complex. There are few Arabs in the news media. And, without a real presence in the news media, Arab Americans have little chance of winning media sympathies. What does that really mean? It means our chances of getting a newspaper editor to assign a reporter to "our" story, or to give "our" story our slant, or to publish "our" story is slim.

And, without "our" story, the news media *is* biased.

Talk about media bias. We used to have a successful Arabic TV program in Chicago called the *Arabic TV Hour*. It was only 30 minutes long!

The news media consists of people. People with personal experiences. People with prejudices. People with a subjectiveness that appears innocently, in most cases, in their understandings and therefore in their writings.

The Middle Eastern Voice was the first effort ever by any Arab American to publish a newspaper founded on the principles of journalism that I was slowly learning while returning to college, this time at the University of Illinois at Circle Campus in Chicago. It was a hotbed of student radicalism and Arab American protests.

Ironically, it was a Jewish professor, Milton Rakove, who took a liking to what he called my "fair-minded approach to the Middle East" and who helped me refocus from a Microbiology Major to American Political Science.

And in helping me better understand Political Science and Chicago Politics, Professor Rakove also helped me focus my energies toward a career in journalism.

I joined the staff of the *Illini* Newspaper. The newspaper office was located between the Arab Student Organization office and the Jewish Student Organization, Hillel. The editor and his assistants had a meeting with me to define what my "role" was to be at the newspaper. I was the first Arab student to join the *Illini* staff and they wanted to make sure that I would be "fair" in my writing.

The editor told me that I would be on "probation" while he assessed whether or not I could, as an Arab student, be "fair."

I happened to be one of the better writers there, although the editors never took a liking to me at all.

I wrote letters to the editor about every aspect of the Middle East, when the editors refused to assign me to stories involving Arab students. I openly advocated the unthinkable, that Israel should negotiate with the PLO and that the Palestinians deserved a state. I also advocated that the Palestinians should recognize Israel and that a good compromise would be a two-state solution with both an Israeli State and a Palestinian State existing side-by-side.

Of course, in true Arab American style, my writings were critical of something. Critical of American policy. Critical of Israel. Critical of the news media. Editorial Page Editors at the *Tribune* and the *Sun-Times* both refused to publish my essay submissions on the Op-Ed Page, where dozens of Israeli commentaries were published unchallenged by articles authored by Arabs.

The only place in the media where an Arab could get published was on the Letter to the Editor page. And, only the "acceptable" parts of a letter from an Arab writer would be published.

I remember in the year before Egypt's President Anwar Sadat went to Jerusalem, I must have sent in 25 letters. Only a few were published by the *Sun-Times*, which clearly had a better record than the Tribune. All of the letters I wrote were critical of Israel, and most were in response to editorials and Op-Ed pieces published by Jewish leaders on the Op-Ed page.

But the week Sadat announced he was going to Jerusalem, I wrote a letter applauding Sadat.

A "Letters to the Editor" Page Editor at the *Sun-Times* called me the next day, excited, and asked, "I just wanted to confirm that you wrote this letter. This is so wonderful. It is great. I am glad you wrote it. We want to run this right away."

I remember hanging up, and repeating to myself, "This is wonderful? It is great? I am glad you wrote it?"

That's supposed to be objective journalism?

I realized then that journalism in America is not objective. In fact, it is subjective, guided by the personal biases of editors, writers, commentators and columnists. And, if you were not part of the journalism "industry," you were not in it.

Most of the letters I had written that criticized Israel had been refused by the editors, or seriously edited. But the one that fit the media's "needs," my letter on Sadat, was applauded and encouraged.

While the Letters to the Editor section is well read and very popular, it carries the stamp of "partisanship" and special interest advocacy.

In other words, most people who read this section expect that many of the views they will read are those of subjective, partisan writers. It is far less prestigious than the Op-Ed or Editorial Pages of a newspaper which carry the imprimatur of journalism and carry a license of presumed authority. Being published on the Op-Ed pages also gave the writer a badge of respectability.

Only a very select few of the Arab leaders were permitted to write commentaries that appeared in the more prestigious pages of the newspaper Op-Ed or Editorial pages. And for every Arab commentary published by the major news media, dozens authored by Jewish writers and community leaders were published.

It was clear the media *was* biased. At least, it appeared that way.

It wasn't that clear that this bias was primarily the result of Arab American absence from the news media profession, more than it was the result simply of anti-Arab or subjective writers and editors.

I realized that the only way to truly advocate my views in the news media was to become a member of the news media.

The Middle Eastern Voice Newspaper was my first effort in that direction. A monthly, *The Middle Eastern Voice* Newspaper survived only 18 issues. The Arab community that complained so often about news media bias, and the lack of pro-Arab writing, failed to pay their advertising bills or to subscribe. They wanted everything free, and they frequently complained when, in the spirit of freedom of expression, *The Middle Eastern Voice* included a viewpoint that they disagreed with. With 22 different Arab countries and more than 100 rival political organizations and parties who rarely saw eye to eye on any issue except opposition to Israel, I was constantly harangued by my own community.

I was the Olympic Swim Competition Gold Medalist criticized for wearing a swim suit.

But that was only the half of it.

I was quickly identified and targeted by the FBI which was actively engaged in the policy and practice of harassing and intimidating Arab Americans.

Despite these problems, I quickly realized the truth of the old saying that the "Arabs have a great case but lousy lawyers, and that Israel had a lousy case and great lawyers." But how we are perceived rests squarely on the shoulders of the different ways in which the Arab and Jewish communities influenced the news media in this country.

The Jewish community influenced the news media.

The Arab American community complained about the news media, denounced the news media, failed to understand the news media, and did not see it as a profession for their children.

Under the Watchful Eye of the FBI

My outspokenness in defense of the Arab American community in Chicago quickly caught the ever vigilant eye of the local office of the FBI.

Telephone calls were plagued by strange noises. Cars that clearly looked like unmarked police vehicles circled my home. People who were once my friend suddenly stopped talking to me.

And, my own paranoia, justified or not, continued to grow.

The truth, I later learned, was that FBI agents harassed my friends, neighbors and business acquaintances.

This happened at a time when the single most fearsome terrorist in the United States was the "Arab terrorist," according to daily news media feedings.

You couldn't turn on a television set or go to the movies without watching some movie where the ugliest, most brutal antagonist was an Arab terrorist. Hundreds of movies carried this theme, and continue today.

Sensing that I was under investigation, and confident that my American citizenship offered me protections that other immigrant Arabs with green cards and residencies lacked, I confronted the problem.

On Nov. 17, 1975, I sent a Freedom of Information request to the US Justice Department in Washington asking if I was under investigation.

If I wasn't under investigation then, I was told by many, I would be now. Asking the FBI if you are under investigation is tantamount to a declaration that you are doing something wrong and want to know if the FBI has become aware of your illegal activities.

Most of my friends and some business acquaintances reported they had been contacted by the FBI concerning my "activities."

As polite as they were, these FBI contacts regarding issues involving international terrorism caused great harm to how people looked at me and at other Arab Americans. Often, we didn't even know about these contacts, or why people suddenly stopped being our friends.

Never mind that I served with distinction in the US Air Force during the end of the Vietnam War and that the FBI had completed a comprehensive investigation of my background when I enlisted in 1973.

Never mind that after being Honorably Discharged from the US Air Force I had enlisted in the Illinois Air National Guard, assigned to the 182nd Airborne in Peoria, Illinois where I served for more than nine years. I later learned that my superiors in the Guard had been informed of my "Arab activities" and I believe it weighed heavily against me, especially when it came time for promotion, I was rejected several times for promotion from the rank of Airman (two stripes) to Sergeant (three stripes).

On July 28, FBI Director Clarence M. Kelley, in Washington, responded in a letter to me that he had no information that I was under investigation and suggested I check with the local office.

I sent several letters. Finally, on May 11, 1977, I sent another Freedom of Information request to the Chicago Office of the FBI asking if they were in fact maintaining a record on me.

On June 1, Special Agent William Beane informed me that I was under investigation, and that the information would be sent to Director Kelley.

That summer, I received a copy of the 25 page FBI report that was being prepared on me.

I was very angry.

After receiving a copy of the report, I wrote Mr. Beane the following letter:

Mr. William F. Beane
Special Agent in Charge
219 S. Dearborn Street
Chicago IL 60604

Dear Mr. Beane:
I was appalled to learn that I was the subject of a local FBI investigation. Obviously, no one in your department here in Chicago bothered to take note from existing government files that I have been an active and loyal member of the United States Air Force and Air National Guard for the past 4 years. A brief examination of my records would have indicated that I have always done my best to serve the interests of the United States.

I find that the only reason that I was investigated was that I am an Arab American and a member of the Arab American Congress for Palestine, an organization with no known connections with any so-called terrorist organization intent on the destruction of the United States. Apparently, the only evidence that you have is your suspicion and obvious belief that the only good Arab is a dead Arab. The attitude and activity of your organization here in Chicago, with respect solely to its activity and harassment of the Arab American community, is anything but commendable.

I wish to inform you that I have brought the entire matter to the attention of Senators Charles Percy and Adlai E. Stevenson, and to Congressman Edward Derwinski of my district. I have also made a complaint to the White House and to my base commander at my Air National Guard Base.

I am not against the right of the FBI to investigate an individual or organization with suspected terrorist connections, but I am against an institutional and endless drive to harass a person or organization simply because they happen to be Arab or Arab affiliated. Aside from the fact that I am an Arab and a member of an organization that has never been officially charged with terrorist activity, your office had no reason to investigate me.

Copies of this letter have been sent along with my complaint to the above mentioned officials.

Sincerely, yours
Raymond G. Hanania

CC: Senator Charles Percy
        Senator Adlai E. Stevenson
        Congressman Edward Derwinski
        President James Carter
        Col. Roland Ballow, Commander, 182nd ANG

Obviously, I was somewhat emotional. But I also was very persuasive.

I sent copies of the letter to my congressional and senate elected representatives demanding redress. I honestly believed that this investigation would be used to influence people against me, particularly in terms of finding employment.

I wanted the report destroyed.

Senator Charles Percy was the first to respond, demanding an explanation from Director Kelley, who wrote me on October 25 that he would review my file based on the Senator's request.

I sent a letter to the President of the United States, too. And Director Kelley immediately wrote back that my letter to the President had been referred to him directly.

On November 11, Special Agent Beane wrote a letter to Senator Adlai E. Stevenson, responding to the senator's demand for an explanation of my circumstances. In the letter, Beane, clearly irritated by my persistence, noted that I had sent similar letters to President Carter, Senator Percy and Congressman Edward Derwinski.

On December 2, Director Kelley wrote me to inform me that the file would not be destroyed.

I appealed the ruling directly to the Office of the US Attorney General. Deputy Attorney General Benjamin R. Civiletti responded several weeks later that they had affirmed Director Kelley's refusal to destroy my file. Mr. Civiletti also confirmed that I was under continued investigation, probably more so now because of all the letters I had written to the dozens of congressmen, my senators and the White House.

Of course, my file was of grave concern to the security of the United States.

I was clearly a "terrorist" and involved in "terrorist" activities.

The FBI claimed that it had begun its "surveillance" of Arab Americans in 1972, after the massacre of 11 Israeli athletes by Arab terrorists.

Well, I guess that justifies it, doesn't it?

Eleven Israeli athletes were murdered in Munich in 1972, so the FBI "had" to investigate my activities as an Arab American. (They could have saved the taxpayers a lot of money simply by requesting my security file from the US Air Force and from the US Air National Guard.)

In 1976, the US surveillance of Arab Americans stepped up and FBI agents actively tried to pressure several Arabs to work as informants. Those that refused were threatened with deportation.

FBI spokesman Ray Wickman who directed the Chicago area surveillance said in an October 30, 1977 Chicago *Tribune* article that the surveillance was necessary to determine if any Arabs were involved in terrorist activities or were members of any terrorist organizations.

He confirmed also that the investigation of Arabs in the United States by the FBI had not turned up one incident or any evidence of Arab involvement or support of terrorist organizations "since 1972."

My FBI file was a treasure chest of sensitive information on Arab terrorist activities in the United States, crucial to the security of the

United States and all good standing and law-abiding Americans.

The copy that they did provide to me was page after page of black magic markered lines, blotting outs paragraphs of surely sensitive information about my terrorist activities in this country.

The report showed that the FBI agents were not stupid, and began with this caution:

"It is believed that an interview of the subject [Ray Hanania] would be unproductive and considering his position as editor of the "Middle Eastern Voice" newspaper mentioned in the enclosed LHM, interview could lead to difficulties in future interviews with other Arab subjects."

You mean like making other Arab subjects aware of their constitutional rights to freedom of expression and civil protections?

If they didn't blacken that paragraph out, which clearly is embarrassing to the FBI, you can imagine how my mind speculated about the content of the dozens and dozens of paragraphs that had been blackened out using a black magic marker.

"Should information come to Chicago's attention indicating that the subject has begun to take part in Arab terrorist activities this matter will be re-opened."

As an American, I feel so secure, now.

The report included a report from the Law Enforcement Agency Data System (LEADS) which was deleted because it was confidential. My photograph was also deleted.

The paragraph that concerned me the most was the one which clearly implied that the report was distributed to other unnamed agencies.

"This document contains neither recommendations nor conclusions of the FBI. It is the property of the FBI and is loaned to your agency; it and its contents are not to be distributed outside of your agency."

That makes me feel real secure.

The document detailed all my vital statistics, most taken from the reverse telephone directory and from the Cook County Recorders

Office and my birth certificate. Individuals were quoted in there providing information about my activities and their names were deleted.

The document also included full page descriptions of terrorist organizations that the document said I was not involved with.

For me, the experience with the FBI was not as traumatic as it was for others.

Born in the United States, more articulate (that's how I was described in my report) than other Arab Americans, I was capable of fighting back.

Other Arabs who protested the FBI's actions were immediately brought before the INS for deportation. Students on green cards or who were residents were threatened and told they would be kicked out of school and expelled from this country.

For doing what?

Expressing criticism of Israel, a foreign country?

This harassment was not based on any foundation of fact. None of the people approached by the FBI were involved in any terrorist activities. If they were, they would have been arrested and prosecuted. But that wasn't the purpose of the surveillance. It was intended as political harassment.

I had learned one lesson, that the FBI and other agencies who were harassing my community feared the scrutiny of the news media.

It was an unusual contradiction in my mind, that the news media which so negatively portrayed my community could also be both our salvation.

I definitely wanted to be a reporter, now.

Journalism Was An Accident
Some Wish I Never Had

The late 60s and early 70s broke up the mix of Arab and Jewish communities in South Shore Valley.

Panic peddling by realtors turned an all-white South Shore Valley into a nearly all-Black community overnight.

I remember the family across the street calling a meeting to urge homeowners not to sell their homes when a Black family rented a home on our block.

Within six months, the family that organized the meeting was the first one to sell. Within months, homes went up for sale and were sold.

It wasn't a matter of racism alone. It had a lot to do with realtors telling people that if they didn't sell their homes today, they would lose all the equity that they had managed to save in their properties.

Interest rates were only 5 percent and selling was simple. The greatest cure to White Flight was the dramatic rise in interest rates in the late 70s and early 80s. A 12 or 13 percent mortgage made it almost impossible for neighborhoods to change overnight.

While nearly all my Jewish friends moved north to Skokie and Niles, nearly all of my Christian friends moved into the Southwest Chicago suburbs, to places like Burbank and Oak Lawn.

Some families moved south, but everyone seemed intent on moving into a suburb outside of Chicago where the homes were cheaper and the schools were new and cleaner.

Whereas Bowen High school was a Zoo. Reavis High school was right out of *Leave it to Beaver*.

I spent my junior and senior years at Reavis High school in

Burbank where I got into more trouble than I got "A's".

It wasn't the first time I had ever heard of "greasers," the combatative restless kids, but I did learn a new stereotype called "dupers," the collegiate class of Christian students with the better grades.

There were hardly any Arab families living in Burbank when we moved in, although they came there in large numbers in the decade that followed.

I really was never focussed on good grades. My poorest achievements were in writing and English composition.

To be honest, writing was never my real goal in life. Journalism was some "typing" course in school, and news was about as boring as watching the afternoon soaps.

Some would say they are not surprised to learn that I had flunked English Composition 101 several times.

In fact, I hated writing. I hated English Lit. I hated spelling.

But it was during my Junior year that I met a visionary teacher whose dedication to her job was memorable and inspiring to me.

Mrs. Harris was the student adviser to *The Reavis Blueprint*. John Fitzgerald was the school's chief administrator. At that time, all I cared about was Grand Funk Railroad and guitarist Eric Clapton.

I had done poorly in English Composition at Bowen High school and at Bogan High school, during Freshman and Sophomore years, and I wasn't about to change for Reavis "The Wrestling Capitol" of the southwest suburbs.

The Reavis Rams were a steamroller and our wrestling team was infamous.

But *The Blueprint* had won its share of awards.

Mrs. Harris knew right away that I was far from a potential quarterback or wrestler, and figured my only hope was to pass English and to stumble into some kind of professional career.

She sat me down in English class one day and asked me what it was that I liked.

I couldn't really tell her, but I did tell her that I could play the *Star Spangled Banner* with my teeth, on my gold Les Paul Guitar -- a Jimi Hendrix talent I picked up watching one of his concerts years before. And, I played guitar for several local bands, even performing at nearby Evergreen Park High school several times.

Instead of kicking me out of class as a hopeless loser, Mrs. Harris suggested that I start writing a column on Rock and Roll music. And my first column was on a new Led Zeppelin album that had just come out that year.

From that moment on, not even Shakespeare could stop my mad dash to turn in my columns.

By Senior year, I had transformed from a 100 pound English Lit weakling to Editor-in-Chief of the Reavis High school *Blueprint*, much to John Fitzgerald's surprise.

I remember during my senior year, I was so enthralled with my budding journalism career that while managing *The Blueprint*, I also served as the editor of an underground student newspaper.

Fitzgerald, who later became Burbank's first mayor after it's incorporation, sat me down in his office, located just outside of the school's garden entrance, and lectured me about running two newspapers at one time.

What bothered Fitz was not that the newspaper was an "underground" publication. What really bothered him was that we used the "F" word in almost every paragraph.

Nowadays, the "F" word is in almost every sentence of every movie, and there isn't anything special about its use, other than that it is still a little classless.

But back then, as a 17 year old, the "F" word was "Freedom."

Fitz convinced me that the underground newspaper still could be a good publication, if we would only remove all the "F" words.

We did, and the *Reavis Underground Newspaper* died an inglorious death.

I can't forget Sergeant Hoop, who nailed me once drinking Malt Liquor in the back of my 1964 Chevy SuperSport with the 409 body and 327 engine superflight automatic transmission with a "stick shift," headers and wide rim tires.

Knocking me on the crown of my head trying to get me to tell him who bought the booze, he kept warning me, "Don't tell me you got it from the doorman at the Red Barn. Don't tell me that."

I didn't.

Neutral dropping on Harlem Avenue over the bridge; drag racing near the forest preserves; the occasional brawl with the Oak Lawn students; Well, it wasn't *American Graffiti*, but it was the next best thing.

There were very few Arab American families in my school back then.

Today, Burbank and Oak Lawn have one of the largest concentrations of Arab American families in the southwest suburbs of Chicago.

But, my journalism career sprouted, and it was during my senior year in college that the editor of the *Southtown Economist Newspaper* decided to give me a job.

Keep Your Views on Your Side of the Typewriter

I remember my first experience interviewing for a job as a newspaper reporter.

The managing editor of *The Southtown Economist Newspaper* was very familiar with my writing. He read my views nearly every week in the Letters to the Editor pages of his newspaper, complaining about and denouncing Israel and Israeli practices against Arabs.

And it was thrown in my face when the editor called and asked me to come in for an interview after I had submitted an application for a job, seven times in the year before.

"You seem to be a good writer," H. Marlin Landwehr began cautiously.

"Thanks, Mr. Landwehr. I know that if you give me the chance, I can do it."

I was worried, though. I believed all that propaganda that the Arabs had thrown at me about the news media being "controlled" by "Jews." The publisher was Jewish and active in Jewish and Israeli causes. Several high profile reporters there were also Jewish.

But then, I figured. Hey. This was the southwest suburbs, after all, and the southwest suburbs were not very sympathetic to ethnics, minorities, Jews or Arabs.

In that mix of discrimination, I felt I had an even chance.

When Landwehr called me back for my final interview, two days later, I couldn't believe I might get the job.

"Dear God. Please. All I want to do is get this job. Please, God. Let me get it. I promise, I will be good." I recited that prayer every step from the parking lot of the newspaper building, at 5959 S. Harlem Avenue. And as I approached the building, I remember standing in awe of the large marque in front: *Southtown Economist Newspapers.*

"God, that's where I wanted to be." I resumed my prayers.

The interview wasn't easy.

"But your resume suggests you never finished college. Why not?"

"Well," I stammered. "I quit Northern Illinois after my sophomore year to join the Air Force because I was about to be drafted into the Army. "When the war ended, I went right back to the University of Illinois, at Circle Campus, and I am finishing up my degree there."

"University of Illinois?" he asked, a smile creeping across his face.

"Well, I am studying journalism and politics. I should graduate in a few months."

"I'm from the University of Illinois. Alumni!" he said.

"I ...," I began.

"We have a lot of U of I alumni here," he said again, his smile getting wider.

His face quickly turned serious again.

"The only problem is that if we hire you ... if I hire you ..."

I thought it was over.

" ... you would have to start next week. I need someone right away. Some of the other reporters seem to like you, and, well, you are a good writer."

"I'll quit school tomorrow," I pledged.

Landwehr leaned back in his chair and then got serious again. "Listen, if you did come on board, you would have to keep your views on your side of the typewriter."

I knew exactly what he had meant, because I had come across that in nearly every turn of my life. No Arab could be outspoken in the United States without being told that they had to keep their own views to themselves.

But it seemed like a small compromise at that moment, with such a major benefit at arm's reach.

"Sure," I lied. "I will."

Quite honestly, Landwehr gave me an opportunity to prove myself. And I appreciated that fact. Arab or not. Although I honestly don't believe he would have hired me back then, in 1978, had my name been Muhammad. Of course, that would have been too much for a newspaper, in an all white suburban community during a time of racial strife, that, at least for a while, had a hard time publishing a picture of a Black man on its front page.

Of course, I tried not to miss an opportunity to write an article about the Middle East.

They did their best to bury them. But, I was a good writer. And, every other reporter at the newspaper also penned personal views about things or issues that directly involved their own lives. The Jewish reporters were the most talented, always writing about the importance of Israel and the Jewish religion. Or, covering Jewish events for the newspaper.

So why should I be different?

My two immediate editors were Jewish. And they quickly tested my objectivity, assigning me to interview holocaust survivors at a meeting of the Decalogue Society, the professional association for Jewish attorneys.

I wondered why I had to cover it. We had no Jewish readers.

I interviewed Simon Weisenthal and diligently wrote about his views on the aftermath of the holocaust and his efforts to track down Nazis, including those who had "escaped and had been given hiding" in Arab countries in the Middle East.

I bit my lip, listened and wrote the story.

It was ironic, in a sense.

Newspapers often stereotype "ethnic" reporters, sending blacks to cover "Black" events, and Hispanics to cover "Hispanic" events, and Jewish reporters to cover "Jewish" events.

But, when it came to sending me to cover an "Arab" event, it was always discussed at length and the decision was always to let someone "more objective" cover the event.

And despite that feeling and as hard as I lobbied, I could never get the newspaper to send a reporter to cover an Arab American event.

"You should really stay away from all that," I was told.

One Jewish reporter who was my editor, told me that he never wrote about anything that he was intimately involved in, including his own religion or community activities.

He was the only one I ever met who practiced what he preached in that regard.

My mom hated the fact that I was a reporter.

I loved it.

I recognized the power of the media immediately, and could see that most Americans only knew about Arabs from what they read in the newspapers.

Arabs, on the other hand, only seemed to react to things when there was something negative published in one of the newspapers.

I figured that as a reporter, I could influence the public, indirectly, and educate them on the real nature of the Arab community. Of course, I got sidetracked into a serious profession covering Chicago politics for some 17 years, and only occasionally wrote about being an Arab.

Mom still didn't understand.

"What if someone get's mad at you, angry with you, and then kills you, *simma-allah*," she would say, clasping her hands to the side of her face. It wasn't a joke with her.

"They'll hurt you."

I tried to explain that being a member of the media protected me from that kind of abuse.

"Mom, not even the mafia would ever murder a reporter. It would cause them all kinds of problems," I would respond.

"*Smis-saleeb wil-alla-azeem*," she would cry out in Arabic.

I had no real idea as to what that meant, but I knew it had to do with asking God for some kind of protection. I'm sure mom wasn't yelling "Damn." I knew all the Arabic swearwords already, and none of them fit.

Of course, being a reporter, attracted the attention of other Arabs in my community and I always tried to work with them to teach them how to approach the media "the right way" and get a positive story in the newspapers about "our cause."

And, that would get me in trouble with the editors.

"You know, you can't be giving advice to people whom you might cover," Landwehr would caution, after calling me into his office.

"I'm not, I was just telling them who to talk to ..."

"You can't be telling them how to do things. You are a reporter. You report the news. You don't make the news."

Tell that to Sam Donaldson, I thought.

Jodi was one of the reporters who had been hired by the Southtown almost a year before me, and who helped tell me how the best way would be to approach Landwehr for a job.

She even gave Landwehr a copy of my resume, and I owed her for helping me to get hired.

On my first day at the newspaper, Landwehr sat me down at a small desk next to Jodi, and near the city editor, George Wurtzinger.

"So, how do you like it so far?" Jodi asked.

"Not bad," I said. "Jodi. Thanks for helping me get hired. I can't believe I'm here."

She said I was welcome. "How much are you making?" she asked quickly.

"Well, he started me at $150 a week. Is that good?"

Jodi's eyes opened wide and her face turned red. And within minutes she was in Landwehr's office.

Seems that there was as much discrimination against women as there was against Arabs.

She was only making $125 a week.

"He said you have a wife and a baby an that's why," Jodi later explained Landwehr's reasoning.

How could I argue?

Her salary did get increased, but she was told not to tell anyone else.

Wurtzinger sat at his desk, chomping on a stogey that danced all day on his lower lip. The bright, hot ashes that dropped from the cigar tip landed on his shirt, some causing small burn marks.

All his shirts were like that.

Wurtzinger called me over and handed me a stack of press releases.

"Retype these and get them back," he barked, handing me the copy.

There was a bright blue Electra-Type typewriter on my desk. I did forget to tell Landwehr one small detail. I didn't know how to type.

But I did quickly learn.

An Artist of Politics

E dward M. Burke was droning on and on about something called the "Bilandic administration" and "urban politics." My right arm was extended across the length of my desk, and my head rested on my folded left arm. My eyes were droning on about Z's.

"Ray. Ray." Milton Rakove gently shook my arm as he quietly tried to wake me from my snooze. "This is important."

Yeah, sure, I mumbled to myself.

Who cares about Chicago politics?

It was January 1976 and I was a junior at the University of Illinois, Chicago Circle Campus ... also recognized as the headquarters for half the student terrorist organizations in Chicago.

I was also president of something called the Organization of Arab Students (OAS), which organized important student activities such as demonstrating against Egyptian President Anwar Sadat's visit with some guy named Richard J. Daley, and protesting the Shah of Iran.

The FBI was compiling a 25-page dossier that began with the insidious caution that they believed I was "involved" in the activities of "several organizations" supportive of Middle East terrorist organizations ... but ended with the buried disclaimer that I was, in reality, "concerned with bettering the Arab American community in Chicago."

I was struggling through a political science major stressing Middle East studies and had taken Rakove's urban politics class to brush off a college elective requirement. It was an up and down year at Circle.

On the positive side, I was invited to debate South African-born former Israeli Foreign Minister Abba Eban (Aubrey Solomon) on Kup's Show.

On the negative side, I was about to be bounced as president of the OAS because my fluency in Arabic was lacking. Other Arab students who opposed my more moderate views, said that I really wasn't an Arab because I didn't speak Arabic fluently. And, quietly, they complained, I was Christian.

Rakove took our class to the ward offices of some guy named Vito Marzullo who lectured us on how politics was a game of relativity -- that is, there was no such thing as good or evil in politics. Everything was measured in relationship to the current context of political events. Politics was personal.

Then he took us to hear some guy named James Taylor, who told us his rags to riches story, and how he later became known as "bulljive" after he allegedly tried to entice sexual favors from a female voter who needed some help.

(It was one of the few times I opened my eyes during those lectures. The other time was when Rakove took us to eat at Vito's favorite Italian restaurant, La Fontanella.)

I didn't know the difference between a committeeman and an alderman, or for that matter, what they did.

I thought City Hall was the place where poor people got married.

But back then, I really didn't care about Chicago politics until Rakove's gentle and insightful teaching style started to grow on me.

Years later, Rakove and I would joke about my original college ambitions. What do you do with a degree in Middle East studies?

Drive a cab?

"It's better to be a terrorist at City Hall covering Mayor Jane Byrne," Rakove would jokingly agree," than be a terrorist eating sand in the Middle East."

Rakove was one of those rare professors who believed that all his students deserved an equal amount of attention and care.

So rather than brush me off as I had his class, Rakove carefully helped me nurture an interest in Chicago politics.

With Rakove's help, I shifted my emphasis from Middle East politics to Chicago politics, learned the difference between a committeeman, alderman and "bagman," got Vito Marzullo's autograph, and convinced the former editor of the *Southtown Economist* Newspapers, H. Marlin Landwehr, to give me a job as a reporter. That was six years ago.

Although Rakove was a University of Chicago student of renowned international political scientist Hans Morgenthau and the theory that power determined politics, Milt Rakove had eternal faith in the better judgement of the public.

Like me, Rakove was sure the public would elect Rich Daley mayor last February. Daley was the best qualified candidate, we thought. We were wrong about one thing. Daley lost.

Rakove put everything into what he did.

"I came to realize after years of teaching, studying and thinking that it is difficult, if not impossible, to understand the nature of politics without immersing oneself in political life," Rakove wrote in his best-selling account of the history of Chicago Machine Politics, *Don't Make No Waves ... Don't Back No Losers.*

So Rakove got involved.

He walked in the St. Patrick's Day Parade, worked as a precinct captain, speech writer and campaign strategist, and even ran for a Cook County office on a "suicide ticket."

Milt patiently passed on those experiences to his students. Though he was considered an "insider", he was objective and he was fair.

"Politics is not a science but, rather, an art," Rakove wrote.

Milton Rakove died Saturday, surrounded by his family. He was 65. He fought a long, hard battle against cancer, something that, unlike my profession, doesn't discriminate between the good and the bad in life.

Politics is an art, Milt, and you will always be remembered, and missed, as one of its finest artists.

(Originally published in the Daily Southtown Economist Newspapers, Nov. 9, 1983. Reprinted with permission, Daily Southtown Economist Newspapers, © 1996.)

Bury Me in Jerusalem

Perception, perception, perception. That is reality in the United States. Success in any ethnic American community, the news media and elsewhere, is just a matter of knowing how to manage perception.

With that basic truth in mind, I found it to be very easy to rise to the top of the Arab-American community.

The "top" wasn't very high.

It wasn't a slow process, either. I moved quickly to the "top," although when I got there, I realized how low we really were when it came to influence and fighting anti-Arab stereotypes.

My motivation to strive to leadership in my community found itself in a military barracks in the middle of a tumbleweed-plagued Idaho desert.

I spent most of my two years in the United States Air Force during the end of the Vietnam War at an F-111 fighter base located stateside, in Mountain Home, Idaho.

I had asked to be sent to Indiana, so I would be close to my family after Basic Training.

But the assignment sergeant made no bones about his dislike for Arabs.

"You want Indiana?" He asked. He knew I was Arab. It was how the training sergeant addressed me the entire six weeks, and the name, "Arab" carried over to Lackland Air Force base where I received training as an emergency medical and dental technician.

"Yes Sir!" I snapped, not veering my eyes or moving my head.

"Well, let's see, Airman Ahab. How about ... Idaho?"

Idaho? I'd never even heard of the place.

I entered training in early October, just before the Egyptian Army under President Anwar Sadat marched across the Nile River and recaptured a sliver of land occupied by the mighty Israeli Army.

It was a major psychological blow to Israel and its supporters, and while it was really a minor military victory, it was a greater moral boost for Arabs around the world.

For the first time, an Arab army had given Israel a black eye.

Of course, that black eye cost me terribly in the service, and it did little to change the world's image of the "Arab," or to "right" the injustice against the Palestinians.

The military didn't treat us like the Japanese during World War II, but they did lecture us about "loyalty."

I knew only two other Arabs while at Lackland, the Assi brothers, twins who had enlisted together and planned to serve together.

Their English was broken, but we often talked and exchanged smiles every time there was a discussion about the Arab attack against Israel.

It wasn't proper to rejoice in the attack against Israel, especially since the Egyptians were still considered a Russian client state, and Israel was America's frontline against the Communist threat against "our" oil fields.

So we rejoiced silently, among ourselves. And we kept quiet when officers or other enlisted personnel spoke about the ghastly "Arab sneak attack" against Israel during its "highest holy days."

During the war, the United States military was placed on high alert. We were told by our base commander that our base was preparing to "assist" if assistance was required.

There was a great fear during those initial days of the 1973 War that the Egyptians would "drive Israel into the sea," even though that was far from the truth or the goal.

But what did truth have to do with perception, anyway?

Everyday, after training, we were called into auditoriums were we received updates on the fighting.

It made Arabs like myself uncomfortable, because in every

discussion, we felt like it was "us" against "them." Our loyalty was always in question, either openly or by virtue of the discussion.

I couldn't believe I would hear that 8th grade question put to me again. "Whose side are you on?"

Hey. I'm wearing an American military uniform and was training to support our fight in Vietnam? What else did you want? My firstborn?

A lot of the African Americans in the service didn't seem so gung ho about supporting Israel, either. My roommates were all Black. I figured that was how the military dealt with integration, by putting minorities and those they perceived as minorities, like Arabs, together in the same barracks areas, two in each room. It was always Blacks together, Hispanics together, and Arabs with everyone. Only the Whites seemed to get rooms with themselves.

The "red necks" were the ones who were most excited about the war, and they wanted to "kick some Arab ass."

I heard the term "sand nigger" so much during the service, and a southern drawl pronounce "Ay-rab!" often.

And the red neck DJ at the bar played Ray Stevens' song "*Ahab the Arab*" often at the Little Egypt strip bar where we hung out after work. When Ray Stevens gets to the part where Ahab the Arab calls his wife, Fatima, or calls his Camel, everyone in the bar starts singing at the top of their lungs, " ... aaaayyyaaaa   yaaaa, yaaaa, aaaayyyaaaa, yaaaa, yaaaa ..."

It was after the war and my training, and during my re-assignment to Mountain Home, Idaho, that I began visiting the base library, reading up on Middle East history.

I was trained as a dental technician, and of course, the new medical base commander felt there must have been some justification to assign me to assist a Jewish dentist. Or, maybe it was coincidence.

Every day in the clinic, we listened intently to "Morris Gindy's" report on the CBS Radio network from Cairo. I taped every report, and would go home and transcribed them, gleaning details and facts.

I recall the doctor mimicking the reporter's sign-off with a heavy Pakistani accent after each report: "This is Morris Gindy. Cairo."

I spent most of my off-duty time at the base library reading every book about the Middle East. I read them all.

And, when I was done, I bought a typewriter and started writing a book that I called *The Palestine Irredentist*, a chronicle of the Palestinian struggle for independence.

My doctor encouraged me, telling me I should reach out to Arab scholars and others for support. I sent letters to everyone, and started to receive replies from people like *Newsweek's* Middle East correspondent Arnaud De Borchgrave.

I remember sending him a letter asking him to review my manuscript, and receiving his Air Mail reply ... Rue de Berrie was the street he lived on in Paris.

I sent the manuscript, 500 pages of history, not from firsthand experience, but an argument, the same argument I was now learning to make with my American friends at the base.

I became somewhat of a "scholar" there and engaged in some detailed discussions about the history of the Middle East, on-the-job education.

They were very interested in the aftermath of the Arab-Israeli war and all the Armageddon hype that followed. The Arab oil embargo and the threats of terrorism all made Middle East discussions interesting.

Letters were coming to the base from all over the world and the Middle East.

And since the letters all are reviewed by the military censors ... they didn't always open them, but they certainly did take notice of the city of origin at one of the country's primary fighter bases ... they began to be noticed.

I received letters from Zehdi Labib Terazi, the spokesman for the Palestine Liberation Organization in New York. Marwan Kanafani, a representative of the PLO, also would send me documents that I would request for my research.

The PLO's office in Beirut would send me photographs, and I received correspondence from offices representing the Popular Democratic Front for the Liberation of Palestine, the Democratic Front, and other organizations, all listed prominently in the United State's Government dossier of known "terrorist" organizations. One letter came from the Headquarters of the Red Cross in Geneva Switzerland, a copy of a transcript of an eyewitness report that followed the 1947 Jewish terrorist attack on the Arab village of Dier Yassin, when followers of Menachem Begin murdered some 252 Palestinian civilians during the first Palestine war.

And, because I believed in fairness, I wrote to Menachem Begin himself, through the Technion in Tel Aviv, asking for his response to charges that he was a terrorist.

Apparently thinking that "Hanania" was a Jewish name, Begin wrote me a short letter telling me he was forwarding me some documentation he thought would help me better understand the conflict and the position of his political organization, the Likud.

I hated the guy but immediately found a bond when I saw his letter was filled with typos, and handwritten corrections in pen.

All coming months after the US and the Soviet Union found themselves near the brink of nuclear war as a result of the Egyptian attack against Israel. Letters with strange postmarks, and sent by organizations blamed for some of the worst terrorist bombings and airplane hijackings in world history.

I guess I should have expected what happened next.

"Airman. What the fuck is going on?"

"Sir?" I asked, not sure what he was talking about.

"I'm talking about all this mail from these organizations all over the world. You think we wouldn't notice?"

"Well, sir. I didn't think there was anything to notice. I am ..."

"Shut up!" He yelled. "And answer when I ask you a question, Airman!"

An airman was the bottom of the pile, one stripe on my sleeve, not even close to being a person until you could reach the lowest rank of sergeant with three stripes.

I finally explained to the base commander that I was writing a book.

"Anti-American propaganda? That could get you a dishonorable discharge, Airman!"

"No sir," I said. "Not anti-American at all."

I explained how I felt, that I needed to understand why so many people were looking at me differently. Why people seemed to hate Arabs.

I needed to understand about my own people.

"You know, some of the other enlistees are complaining about you staying up late and typing your manuscript. We are concerned about it."

I had to give him a copy. He read it and returned it with a note that simply read, "Interesting."

When the Vietnam War ended in 1975, I was one of the first enlistees to be offered a discharge through a program called Palace Chase. They said they simply didn't need all of us anymore and we could trade in our remaining years of active duty assignment for service in an Air National Guard base near our homes. We would receive two years Guard duty for every year of active duty remaining. I had two years left in my enlistment.

As soon as I reported in to my Guard base, the 182nd Airborne Unit, Peoria, Illinois, the base security officer called me into his office and lectured me about "causing trouble."

I couldn't believe it.

The more I hit this wall, the more I wanted to break through.

Out of active duty and only required to drive to Peoria once each month, I had a lot of time to go back to school and strengthen what I had learned about the Middle East while in the service.

And I desperately wanted to reach out to my own community.

I knew they were around. I just had to find them.

I started by writing letters to the editor of local newspapers on my own.

At first, my letters to the Chicago *Sun-Times* and the *Tribune* were routinely rejected.

I'd read all these letters from people attacking the Arab cause, and very few from Arabs defending it.

But little by little, my letters started to get in.

One day, Professor Ibrahim Abu-Lughod at Northwestern University called me and asked me to attend a meeting of an organization called the Arab-American Congress for Palestine.

I was really excited, especially since I had read many of Abu-Lughod's books on Palestine and its history called "*The Transformation of Palestine*," the bible on Palestinian history.

He was a political icon in my community, someone I really admired, and probably the most eloquent spokesman for the Arab cause in the world. And he was one of two chief motivators to push PLO Chief Yasir Arafat to pursue peaceful negotiations with Israel in the late 1980s. He never received the notoriety that he deserved, and while he probably shunned it, it could have allowed him a platform to further champion the Arab cause.

So I decided I'd prepare for the meeting, which was held in a small storefront banquet hall located on Kedzie Avenue at 59th Street, which was then the heart of Chicago's South Side Arab community.

I wanted to fit in. It was my first meeting. So I unwrapped a red and white *Keffiyeh* that my mom had kept in a closet, and placed it on my head. I fit the black rope around the crown to hold it in place and flipped one of the ends across the chin and over my left shoulder.

I looked like Yasir Arafat. Although most Americans thought all Arabs looked like Arafat even without the traditional Arab headdress on their heads.

It took a lot of nerve on my part to drive from my home in Burbank the two miles through Chicago to the meeting location.

I parked across the street, and with the red and white *Keffiyeh* on my head, I waked into the banquet hall room.

The speaker at the front of the hall stopped and watched me as I entered, and everyone turned around and stared, as if they had never seen a spectacle like that before.

They were all in suit pants and white shirts, blue collar shopkeepers who had just closed their stores and were interested in news about what was happening in the Middle East.

And I sat there the whole evening, struggling to understand the very difficult Arabic that was being spoken. If they had been talking about the evening meal, I would have understood. But this was politics, and the words were things I had never heard my mother and father speak before.

Sihyuneen was Arabic for Zionist. Politically correct Arabs referred to the Israelis as *Sihyuneen*, which means Zionist, not *Yahudi*, which means Jew, both in Arabic.

My mom never called the Israelis "Zionists." The term meant nothing to her. She called them by the term they called themselves, Jews. "The Jews did this ... The Jews did that." To the outsider, it might sound anti-Semitic. But my mother wasn't anti-Semitic at all and was probably the most kind heart that ever lived.

But Americans who heard Arabs speak often took the use of the word "Jew" to be derogatory and anti-Semitic.

I still have a hard time using the word "Jew" because it sounds so harsh. Conditioning, really. I have to say "Jewish." And, when talking about politics, I have to say Israeli or Zionist, although the latter term lost its luster as peace slowly crept upon the Fertile Crescent.

Within two weeks after that meeting, I found myself helping the Congress prepare its press releases. In fact, I helped them prepare their first press release, announcing an event where we planned to bring some Middle East speakers.

I sent it to all the newspapers.

Not one of the press releases ever made it into print. No mention in Kup's column. No mention of activities to come in the Community Calendars.

I tried to explain to my new friends that politics was fine but "preaching to the choir" was non-productive.

"We should be talking to the American people," I would argue. "They're the ones who need to hear what we have to say."

"But the media is controlled by the Jews" was the quick response and "no one will publish our views." I understood the logic, but it was wrong.

So, I decided to start my own newspaper, in English, called *The Middle Eastern Voice*.

And I also volunteered to serve as an English announcer on a radio program called *The Voice of Palestine*.

It all seemed so important, back then. The newspaper, the radio reports. But I still felt we were losing the battle and the war.

I'd watch our representatives on television lose every debate, every time.

Their arguments were correct. They just didn't look good presenting them.

And I didn't listen to the arguments. I watched and compared how the Arab and Israeli representatives acted.

In fact, the first time I really was moved was watching an Arab and Israeli debate on Kup's show that was picked up by a local television station in Mountain Home Idaho, while I was in the service. I sat in the front room of the single bedroom mobile home anchored in the middle of the Idaho desert and screamed at the TV.

I knew more than that guy. The Arab looked like an idiot. All his college diplomas, degrees and titles couldn't make up for how poorly he presented himself on TV.

The Israeli spokesman was always dressed like an American, always speaking perfect English. His suit was sharp, the tie was fashionable and his hair was always so perfectly cut.

They always had cool names, like "Howard Squadron." It sounded so tough.

The Arab, on the other hand, dressed so sloppy. Because to Arabs, image didn't matter more than the principle of the ideology.

How absurd to think that perception was greater than the principle. We ignored perception and tried so hard to document every dotted "I" and every crossed "t."

His name was something that sounded like part of Ray Stevens' song, "*Ahab the Arab.*" It might as well have been Hubble-Bobby Al-Boobah Ali!

In some parts of the United States, they put you in jail for having a name that sounded like that.

The Arab "argument" in these debates was so predictable. It was one of loud emotion. Incoherent logic, drowned in footnotes, explanations, and historical insignificance.

Did you ever read a novel written by an Arab? There are as many pages of notations in the back as there are pages in the book. It is as if we Arabs have to continually justify our arguments. And, anyone who knows anything about a public debate knows that those people who try the hardest to justify their arguments always come across like they are lying.

Even Professor Abu-Lughod's book, *The Transformation of Palestine,* is filled with footnotes. (Read the book *Exodus.* No footnotes. Yet more Americans believe what they read in *Exodus* than they do in the more accurate *The Transformation of Palestine.*)

The individual, on the other hand, who makes his case calmly, consistently and without trying to "convince" an audience of its veracity is the individual an audience most often identifies with.

I knew how to do it.

And one day, I got my chance.

"Mr. Hanania?" the voice on the telephone asked.

It was a woman, calling. Someone very distinguished.

"Yes," I answered.

"This is Esse Kupcinet."

Until then, I had no idea who Kup was. I recall seeing his TV show in Idaho, while in the Air Force. He was just some columnist at the *Sun-Times* who always wrote about Israel. He also hosted a weekly television show that was broadcast all across the country on public television.

I knew he was ferocious about his defense of Israel. And that usually meant being unfair to Arabs.

"I understand that you are the spokesman for the Arab-American Congress," Esse said. In all the time we ever spoke, neither she nor Kup would ever say the word "Palestine."

"The Arab-American Congress *for Palestine*," I emphasized.

"Right. We would like to invite you on our program to talk about the developments in the Middle East with Abba Eban. Can you make it?"

Could I make it? Television? A national audience. Damn right I would be there.

At the TV station, Kup and Eban spent a lot of time talking together in the studio. Esse escorted me to a green room where I sat alone until I was called onto the set.

It as the first time I had ever done TV. But I knew my mission. I wasn't going to scream and ˠ ll. I wasn't going to try and fill the 22 minutes of the half hour shuw with a six-hour argument about the history of Palestine.

No, Eban was too smart for that. And Kup certainly would not miss the chance to join in a tag team pummeling of another Arab spokesman, even one as young as me.

I remember the introduction. Kup went on and on about the achievements of Abba Eban, Israel's foreign minister and the Jewish State's most eloquent spokesman.

Kup simply turned to me, and in the only broken English spoken that night, announced, "And we also have, Ray Ha-na-nana ..."

"Hananeeya," I corrected.

"Hananeeya," he repeated with some emphasis, "the spokesman for the Arab-American Congress."

"... *For Palestine*," I corrected with a smile.

Right away the mild mannered Eban shot off on a tangent about the *Benelux* system of government and how it was impossible to believe that Jews and Arabs -- he never said Palestinians -- could not share the same land. The *Benelux* system was an unusual form of government that linked Belgium, the Netherlands and Luxemborg. (Get it, Benelux. Fortunately, I had come across the term during my readings at Mountain Home Idaho.)

Eban went on and on about how "tiny Israel" was faced with annihilation, surrounded by 22 hostile Arab countries all bent on driving the "tiny Israel" into the very large Mediterranean sea.

Finally, after Kup and Eban started stroking themselves for the first 5 minutes of the show, I interjected, "I don't know about the *Benelux* system, at all. All I know is that my father was born in Jerusalem."

Eye contact. I remembered the single rule of successful television, and I stared at the camera trying to make "eye contact" with the TV land audience, instead of looking at Kup or Eban.

And I wanted the TV audience to see "puppy eyes" on the brink of tears, rather than the usual serving of emotional, screaming, wild Arab propaganda.

"My father was ... sniffle, sniffle ... born in Jerusalem and ... sniffle, sniffle ... he can't go back to his home." He had died by then. But a point was a point. "And, I am his son ... sniffle, sniffle ... and I can't go back to my father's home ... sniffle, sniffle ... My grandfather's home. And my great grandfather's home."

And then, I looked at the distinguished looking Abba Eban, relaxed, calm and collected, on the seat next to me, beaming with the confidence of 2,000 years of successful debates and military victories. And I said, "The distinguished Abba Eban can go there anytime he wants, even though he was born in South Africa, and his real name is Aubrey Solomon."

I could hear Essee Kupcinet croak behind the lights of the studio, and Kupcinet immediately jumping to Eban's rescue.

Eban's relaxed demeanor suddenly snapped to attention. He sat up straight and his knees came together tight. His face turned stern, and I never got another word in edge wise.

Body language said it all.

"I can arrange to have you return to Israel," Eban responded.

"What about the 3 million other Ray Hanania's?" I asked.

"What is it that you want, Mr. Hananana?" Kup asked, coming to Eban's defense. Kup argued that "I" had 22 Arab countries to choose from to move to. Why did I want to move to Israel?

"I just want to be buried where my father was born," I said softly, with piercing aim.

And without losing a beat, Kup responded with a wink to Abba Eban, "I think we can take care of that."

Neither Esse nor Kup said goodbye, and an aide escorted me to the door. I did manage to get Eban to give me an autograph, though, as I was being ushered out.

As I waited at the light to cross Michigan Avenue to catch a bus and return home, I saw Eban relaxed in his long, black chauffeur-driven limousine, waiting at the same light. Eban was smoking a cigar. He just stared at me as I stood at the curb.

Most of the people who saw the show thought I did well. Instead of dragging the TV audience into a murky argument over politics and history, I had turned it into a personal story that the public could easily identify with.

But right away, I heard from the Arab "leaders," who complained that I had made some comments that seemed to support the PLO and Yasir Arafat. And back then, the Arab community was divided, here in the United States, between those who supported Arafat, a "moderate" revolutionary, and George Habash, an "extremist" revolutionary.

"Why didn't you tell them about how the Jews murdered our people? Or about how the Jews control the media. Or about ..."

It went on and on for weeks.

Now, I monitored Kup's column daily and found that he wrote about Israel and the Jewish community nearly every week.

I wrote Kup a letter and asked why he didn't mentioned items of interest involving the Arab community, and noted that I had just become a father and had named my daughter "Haifa" after a port city in Palestine that was now part of Israel.

"Well, if you have a son, will you name him Jerusalem?" Kup wrote.

Later, Kup and I became very good friends when I was hired as a reporter at the *Southtown Economist* and later at the Chicago *Sun-Times*, where Kup worked too. I always favored Kup with items from the City Hall beat, and he appreciated it. (The editorial faces at the *Sun-Times* had changed significantly, by then, too.)

He never did loosen up his style of ignoring the Arab community, but occasionally he would mention when I would reach some achievement in my community.

The point was that Kup never turned an item down that I gave him. But he didn't go out of his way to find "scoops" about the Arab community.

Not giving in, I completed my manuscript and gave the final draft to Professor Abu-Lughod for review.

I remember Abu-Lughod giving it serious review, but telling me quite frankly, "It's a great book, Ray. Really. Very well written. Well noted. Good research. But, Ray, really. No one will publish it. Who is Ray Hanania? It's good, though."

Making it Big Time

The call from Mary Dedinsky came out of the blue, the same way every achievement I ever cherished materialized.

"Ray, I don't understand it, but Ken wants you in here now. Can you do it?" Dedinsky asked, calling from the *Sun-Times* office. It was only four weeks before that efforts to secure an interview, with Mary's help, had been politely put off.

Ken Towers was the managing editor of the Chicago *Sun-Times*. In 1985, he was the man to see if you wanted a job at the newspaper, and the *Sun-Times* is where I had longed to be. As a community newspaper reporter working under the shadow of the *Sun-Times'* venerable City Hall Dean, Harry Golden, Jr., the *Sun-Times* was *the* newspaper in Chicago.

I was ready to move from the *Southtown Economist* Newspapers where I had worked as City Hall reporter for nearly 8 years. And they were ready for me to move, too. *Southtown* Publisher and socialite Bruce Sagan had called me and five other senior reporters into a meeting and basically told us that we could no longer expect any additional raises.

"I would be happy to give you all references to find new jobs," Sagan said coldly, explaining in his business, the bottom line was money. At that time, I was highest paid reporter at the *Southtown*, making more than $450 a week to write the *Political Grapevine* column and to cover Chicago's City Hall.

But leaving wasn't easy. For more than a year, I had sent out resumes to newspapers all over the country, and in the Chicago area.

The *Sun-Times* and *Tribune* simply sent me form letters saying "no." Many others did not even reply.

Several weeks before Dedinsky's call, I had received a job offer from a Copley Newspaper, *The Herald News*, in Joliet.

The editor there offered me a job and promised me that I would have an opportunity to develop a political column once I got my feet wet covering Joliet. Best known for its prison, Joliet is located about 40 miles Southwest of Chicago in Will County.

It was better than nothing, larger than the *Southtown*, but still a step away from my goal, the big time daily newspapers like the *Tribune* and *Sun-Times*.

I dutifully turned in my resignation letter to Sagan and was saying goodbye to friends at City Hall. Alderman Edward M. Burke, probably the most articulate member of the Chicago City Council, introduced a resolution "roasting" me, but noting my departure as another event in City Hall history.

One after another, Chicago aldermen stood up and lambasted me, ridiculed me, criticized me, but wished me well at my new job.

"I'm happy to see Ray move on," said Burke's colleague Ed "Fast Eddie" Vrdolyak. "Good riddance." Vrdolyak was the leader of the Vrdolyak 29, rebel aldermen who fought the takeover of the City Council by the newly elected mayor, Harold Washington, Chicago's first African American mayor.

Even Washington rose to the occasion, joining in the roast. While the roast was all in fun, only hours earlier, the City Council had engaged in a bitter battle to embarrass a key Washington ally, Ald. Dorothy Tillman.

Tillman was a street fighter and a symbol of African American oppression, fighting back against the white establishment. The Vrdolyak 29 had voted to block every appointment Washington had made, trying to force him to compromise on other issues.

Tillman had thumbed her nose at Vrdolyak and his rebel colleagues by refusing to remove her hat when she took her seat at the council meeting. It was City Council tradition that aldermen remove all head coverings when entering the City Council chamber out of respect. Of course, that rule was made by men when the council was all-men. And, with the city's first woman mayor leaving office and being replaced by the city's first African American mayor, old traditions were fast being broken.

I was the first Arab American reporter ever to cover Chicago politics, and to cover City Hall. During the Tillman battle, Washington gave her a dozen red roses as a welcome gesture. He desperately needed votes on the council. Tillman was allowed to keep her hat, but only after Vrdolyak's allies rose to denounce her as a troublemaker and a disgrace to the aldermanic profession.

It was during my roast that Tillman rose to criticize me as a typical White reporter who was insensitive to the concerns and needs of African Americans (it wasn't true, and she was joining in the spirit of the roast). Afterwards, she walked over to me in the press box and, in a symbol of goodwill and best wishes, handed me one of her 12 roses. It was always a time to celebrate when Tillman could help usher a "white" reporter out of the City Hall press room, one reporter observed.

That might have ended there except a very observant reporter for the Chicago *Sun-Times*, who, writing a story about Tillman's battle with the Vrdolyak 29, noted in his story that Tillman had presented me with a rose.

And, that's how Ken Towers found out that I was leaving, prompting him to direct Dedinsky to call me and ask me to come in for an interview immediately.

Towers was very direct and offered me a job as one of four reporters who were to work on a new column he had created called Page 10. Page 10 was a personality column, similar to what I had been writing at the *Southtown*. The *Sun-Times* wanted to counter the popularity of a much more gossipy column at the Chicago *Tribune* authored by former Mayor Jane Byrne's press secretary, Mike Sneed.

I jumped at it, although I explained to him that I was starting a job with the *Joliet Herald News* and would have to notify them that

I would not be able to start my new job there the following Monday.

Towers sat me down with several reporters who he said I would be working with, political writer Lynn Sweet, TV and Radio writer Robert Feeder, Features Editor Carol Stoner and features writer Marla Paul.

"Look Ray, I know you're an Arab," one editor advised jokingly after the meeting. "They're all Jewish. Don't start a war there."

For two years, I worked on the column covering politics. It was a tortuous column because while it was given the highest priority and the highest visibility in the newspaper -- our pictures as a team where promoted in full color on the sides of the hundreds of *Sun-Times* delivery trucks -- it also had the largest kitchen full of chefs. Everyone wanted to tell us what to write and how to write it.

Everyday, an item would come down from an editor or the publisher promoting some personal event or achievement.

It was still very well read.

The interview with Towers wasn't my first experience at the *Sun-Times*.

Years earlier, as a cub reporter for the *Southtown Economist* Newspapers, I had received a call from *Sun-Times* columnist Roger Simon.

Simon was a very good columnist, but whenever he wrote a story about the Arab or Jewish communities, he was always biased against us. No one in my community liked him.

But I took the call because he began the conversation with me talking about journalism and asking how I liked my job at the *Southtown*.

Simon asked me if I had attended a meeting that had taken place between leaders of the Arab community and the Rev. Jesse Jackson, Jr. Simon made it clear to me that if I helped him with the "Jackson-Arab story," I might curry favor with the *Sun-Times* editors and land myself a job there.

I said yes, but that the meeting was private and I did not want to be quoted. I asked him what he had heard.

At the meeting, Jackson, whom I had admired, had bluntly told Arab leaders that he would help them, but they had to help him raise money for his organization, Operation P.U.S.H.

I was invited because I was still very close to the city's Arab leadership, and I was lobbying them to pay more attention to public relations, image and the news media, instead of to political issues and ideology, which consumed all their efforts.

Jackson left that meeting raising more than $10,000 from the Arab businessmen, and he promised in return to champion the Arab cause.

He said he had worked for years closely with the Jewish community, but some how, that relationship had soured. His Jewish support was evaporating and he said we, Arabs, could fill that void.

I agreed to answer Simon's questions because I honestly believed that Simon would be fair.

I also needed that entre to meet with the *Sun-Times* managing editor at that time, Stuart Loory, Towers' predecessor. I confirmed much of what Simon already knew, and, as he promised, he arranged a meeting for me with Loory the following week.

But that weekend, Simon's story hit the newsstands. It was a very negative attack against Jackson, asserting he was selling himself as a spokesman for the Arab cause in exchange for money. Simon kept quoting his "Arab source who attended the meeting."

Simon was a frontline doberman for the Jewish community. His columns were intended to enlighten the world about Jewish community achievements and champion their fight against the Arab viewpoint. And, in my opinion, he was viciously unfair to Arab Americans.

Years earlier, Simon authored several columns which associated an Arab restaurant owner in Skokie as a supporter of the PLO.

Hamid Barbarawi owned a small but popular *falafel* house on Dempster, and he advertised his business on the Palestinian radio program that I had worked on as a volunteer, called *The Voice of*

Palestine Radio, which was sponsored by the Arab American Congress for Palestine.

That was the basis for the so-called link Simon made between Barbarwai and the PLO.

The Voice of Palestine Radio was clearly anti-Israeli and reported frequently on Middle East politics with a pro-Palestinian slant, in much the same way that Roger Simon often wrote about Middle East politics, but with a pro-Israel slant. Israel, Palestinians and the Arab world *were* at war.

Simon's columns so injured Barbarawi that he eventually closed his restaurant after many Jewish customers boycotted his business. He eventually dropped his ads on the radio program, too.

Leaflets saying much more nastier things about Barbarawi, and some based upon Simon's columns, made their way through the streets of Skokie. Simon offered a defense of the leaflets asserting that "some people" suspected that Barbarawi had printed the leaflets to win sympathy in his fight to stay open.

Simon's column served to insure that Barbarawi's efforts to enlist police help to investigate the harassment failed.

Much like the Jews who were chased out of Germany before World War II, Barbarawi was chased out of Skokie. And Simon was partly responsible.

It was an ugly, hateful event that nobody seemed to care about, and it further motivated me to pursue my dream of a media job.

I wanted that *Sun-Times* job because I believed that Arab Americans could never influence the news media from the outside as successfully as others were doing it from the inside.

I didn't want to be biased as Simon was in this instance. I wanted the media to be fair.

By the time Towers had offered me the Page 10 job, Simon had departed. My original motivation to become a reporter had changed from one of politics to one of profession.

I loved being a journalist and I believed strongly in being objective.

Getting the Arab American story out to the American people did not require being biased.

In my 17 years as a reporter, I had only authored less than two dozen articles on Arab American or Middle East issues, far less than the articles that had been written by Jewish reporters on Israel or Jewish related subjects.

Working at the *Southtown* taught me that objective journalism was much more effective than slanted reporting.

It became clear to me that one of the major problems facing Arab Americans was not so much that the reporting about us had been biased, but that the reporting was incomplete and lacked our views.

In March 1985, when I was walking from City Hall along the Chicago River bank to the *Sun-Times* building at 401 N. Well Street, I prayed openly. "Please God, just give me this job. I won't ever ask for anything else." (It was the same prayer I had offered when interviewing at the *Southtown*.)

Page 10 was a blast. When I wasn't covering some political event, I was covering a movie star.

Actress Cloris Leachman had arrived in town and Carol Stoner asked me to do a short item on her for Page 10.

When I arrived at the Drury Lane in Oak Brook, four other reporters were waiting in line ahead of me.

By the time I got to meet Leachman, she was tired.

"Listen, Miss Leachman. What more can you tell me that you haven't already told everyone else?" I asked.

She smiled and started telling me how tired she was of interviews and wished she could get out of doing this one with me.

"All I want to do is go shopping," she said with a deep sigh.

"Well, why don't we just go shopping, then?" I asked.

We jumped in her limousine and drove out to a very chic boutique on Oak Street called Ultimos.

Ultimos is where the very rich romped, because the rich didn't have to "shop."

They bought what they saw.

Leachman danced around the two story boutique trying on everything, stripping her clothes off in front of me and making me blush with one eye open.

She was very good looking and I was still young.

She picked out clothes, jewelry and other items and as I stood at a table admiring a jade bracelet, she asked if I liked it.

"Hey, it looks okay to me."

"Then I'll take it," she told the woman assigned by the boutique to help her shop.

When we went over the shopping list, the bill came out to be just over $6,000. The bracelet I happened to notice that prompted her to buy cost almost $2,000 alone.

I wrote a short item detailing the shopping spree and the cost.

It was fun. Page 10 also gave the Chicago Bears' lineman William Perry the nickname "The Fridge."

Of course, not everything was fun.

When Paul Newman and Tom Cruise were in Chicago filming the *Color of Money*, an assistant producer I had met on the set called me with an item he thought would be funny for our column.

According to the producer, they were having a hard time filming Cruise shooting hard-to-make pool shots.

I and a partner on the column at that time, Mary Gillespie, tried in vain to get Cruise to respond to an item we decided to run. It noted that Cruise was supposed to be the next generation's Paul Newman, but he wasn't a good pool player. Stand-ins were required to make the more complicated pool shots.

When the story appeared in the paper the next day, our publisher called and yelled at me for embarrassing him.

"Newman is invited to a dinner at my house tonight and what am I supposed to say?" he yelled. *The Color of Money* was somewhat of a sequel to Newman's earlier hit classic, *The Hustler*. In it, he reprised his role as "Fast Eddie" Felson, a retired pool hall hustler who became a mentor to the younger hustler played by Cruise.

The truth, I thought, meekly listening as the *Sun-Times* publisher raked me across the coals. I understood his embarrassment.

Later that week, we received a letter addressed to both of us from Newman which read simply:

> *I know you guys are above embarrassment, but you will label yourselves as first-class, working assholes when you see Tom Cruise shoot pool in THE COLOR OF MONEY.*
>
> *Whenever the chance arises to point out instances of media inaccuracy, I will make a point of mentioning you by name.*

(Newman had already finished another successful film on the sleazy side of journalism with Sally Field called *Absence of Malice*, which was my defense in this instance.)

As my role at Page 10 increased, my appearances on TV and on radio increased too.

And, I quickly caught the ever vigilant eye of Chicago's most renowned image maker, Paul Glick.

The popularity of Paul Glick's coiffure put him on the "A - list" of people invited to all the socialite parties.

And since I was the "A - list" keeper, at that time, Glick called me up one day and offered to give me a preliminary "make-over."

"If you want to be someone in this town," Glick explained, "you have to dress the part."

It started with an analysis that took about two hours at Glick's Gold Coast offices.

"Ray. The big problem with you is that, as an Arab, you have dark skin. Your dark hair and eyes are very attractive to the public, but if you are not careful about how you look, you come across in a sinister way to them," Glick explained.

"If you are not careful, you could project that image to the public. Perception, in this country, is reality."

I had heard that many times and it later became the foundation of my media consulting philosophy.

Glick advised me that I had to off-set this negative (Arab) projection by always wearing white shirts, keeping my hair cut very short, eliminating my mustache (that I had since I was 13), and working on my articulation and enunciation.

He could help redefine me, for a mere $12,800, according to his calculations.

I decided against buying the make-over but did not reject his ideas at all.

The session was informative and I wrote a short item about the experience for Page 10.

And I immediately went out and bought 10 very crisp white shirts. I refused to shave off the mustache but I had my hair cut at his coiffure. A regular stylist cut cost $18.00 on the street. His bill was $32.

A small price to pay for image, I thought.

I Sent My Aunt a Letter

The closeness of the Palestinian community is best described by a hand written letter.

The letters my mom wrote to her sister, Leila, who lives in a town called Ramallah in the West Bank were different than the letters she sent to everyone else.

Different in physical appearance.

The paper was soft and thin. The light weight helped reduce the cost of postage.

It was marked *Air Mail* in red and the color of the paper was light blue.

The postage was higher than normal postage for letters sent to destinations in the United States.

But, the US Post Office took several steps to reduce costs and keep the letter's weight down.

First, the paper was extra thin. So thin, you could almost see through it.

And, the letter was like something someone had cut out in an elementary school art class. It was a single sheet of paper shaped like a cross.

Mom would write in Arabic on each of the little panels, inside and out. And, when she was done, she would fold it up. Pre-glued edges that folded over, let her create an envelope and seal most of the contents.

My family, like other Palestinian families, always made a big deal out of the address.

If the letter did not have the country "Israel" written on the outside, the letter would not be mailed.

Oftentimes, dad would write letters addressed to his relatives in

Jerusalem, "Palestine."

And, the Israelis would simply send it back, stamped, "No Such Address" in English, or "Return to Sender."

It was an inexpensive protest. But, it did mean that the letters never made it to their destinations.

Sometimes, dad would affix a Palestinian souvenir stamp to the letter. And, of course, that came back even quicker.

These returned letters made great souvenirs.

Protest or not, mom and dad still had to get a letter to their families back home.

So, on every letter, mom would rewrite, Jerusalem "Via Israel" or Ramallah, "Via Israel."

The "Via Israel" was a quiet form of protest, a compromise the Israelis would accept.

Many times, letters from back home arrived with a small red stamp placed on it by the Israelis that read, simply, "Censored."

The letters were opened by the Israelis, read, re-sealed and sent on their way, if they didn't mind what was being written.

There was no promise that a letter going or coming from Palestine would ever make its destination.

So, I would often listen to my mom on her occasional, long distance telephone calls to my aunt, spending half the conversation talking about the letters they sent that didn't make it.

Of course, they also knew that their telephone conversations were being tapped by the Israeli *Shin Bet* (secret service) too.

It was the same when mom and dad would travel back home.

They couldn't allow the Israelis to stamp their passport, because the Israeli Immigration Stamp in their passport would invalidate it for any other Arab country.

After all, my dad would explain, the Arab World was at war with Israel and it was legitimate to demand that the stamp be placed on a separate piece of paper that would accompany the US Passport as it made its way from Israel to other Arab countries.

The problem, however, was that mom and dad never did visit any other Arab countries the entire time since they had left Palestine.

They really didn't need the "outside stamp" because no other Arab Immigration Officer would see their passport anyway.

But, that wasn't the point.

(My dad was very American, and Americans are fond of noting, "That isn't the point.")

And, it wasn't the point for mom either.

Every time mom or dad would go back home, they would return with their unstamped passport, the Israeli Immigration Slip tossed out at O'Hare Airport after returning from Israel.

Mom didn't have to keep an address book with the addresses of her relatives, either.

I thought it was a protest, too. But it wasn't.

My Aunt Leila's address was:

Habib Al-Hin
Main Street
Ramallah, Via Israel.

The "Via Israel" was always underlined, to set it apart from the rest of the address.

I always thought Main Street was some small little street and that Ramallah must have been a tiny village.

But, when I arrived there in later years, I discovered what I had already suspected, that Ramallah was this huge metropolis and that Main Street was several miles long.

"Habib Al-Hin, Main Street, Ramallah?"

How on Earth did the postman get the letter to its destination.

As it turns out, everyone back home knows everyone.

In fact, years after my Uncle Habib had passed away, the letters were still addressed to his name, to guarantee that they would reach my aunt and her three sons.

My parents always cherished the letters they had received from back home.

It was an event. Not trivial. Something the entire family participated in.

Everyone would sit around my mother and she would slowly read each word in the letter, savoring each syllable and sound.

The letter had fewer than 500 words, scribbled and cramped as closely as possible to fit on the single sheet paper. But it took forever for the letter to be read.

My dad once compared it to sitting around the family radio listening to FDR offer a fireside chat from the White House.

Dad loved FDR.

The experience of those moments are gone forever, not just because the significance of these letters had died with my parents. But because of the rapid development of technology.

I just don't recall the last time my daughter and I sat around my IBM ThinkPad Portable Computer, reading the frequent E-mail messages sent "Via the Internet" from my cousins in Ramallah.

It's hard to make a subtle protest on the Internet.

It just isn't the same.

A West Bank Story:
In Search of Palestine

(Just around Christmas in 1989, I received a single page letter from my mother's sister who lives in Ramallah, a large, predominantly Christian Arab city in the Israeli military occupied West Bank. The letter was hand written and it was very painful to read.

(My aunt wrote about how difficult life was under the Israeli military occupation. As I read, I looked at the envelop and saw that an Israeli military "censorship" stamp had been placed on the front bottom corner, indicating that the contents of the letter had been read by military censors.

(My aunt wrote ...

("....about our news, we are all in good health till now, in spite of the times that we were beaten many times in our shop and house and in the street by the Jewish soldiers. Imagine, dear Ray, that I am, your aunt, had been beaten many times by the Jewish soldiers in the street while I was trying to save some children and babies who were terrified from the gun shots and bombs and from the gas bombs. There is an Arabic saying, `the one who leaves his house is lost. And the one who returns is newly born.' By these words I summarize the situation in our Palestine ...."

(I read that letter over and over again, and one day showed it to my editor. He suggested I make copies and show it to other editors and even some reporters at the newspaper, which I did. In 1990, tensions had heightened when Iraq invaded Kuwait and the Middle East was the focus of much news and world attention. And in the

fall, I had asked if the Chicago Sun-Times would sponsor a trip by me to the Middle East to offer a perspective on the preparations for what appeared to be an American-led invasion of Iraq and apprehensions in Israel and the occupied est Bank.

(Now, I was the only reporter at the newspaper of Arabic heritage. In fairness to the Sun-Times, I was the only newspaper reporter of Arabic heritage at any Chicago area newspaper. There were dozens of reporters who were Jewish, including several editors. Although sympathetic, the newspaper's editors rejected my request, even when I countered that they had sponsored trips taken by several Jewish reporters who, on their return, wrote lengthy articles about life in Israel. Every year, I added, we did a special insert on Israel's birthday. And, we had a Jewish, Israeli citizen who offered our only firsthand weekly coverage of the Middle East. We had no Arab reporter to counterbalance his reporting, which I felt was partisan.

(Eventually, I was given a leave-of-absence and I paid for the trip myself. When I returned, I submitted five stories. The editors agreed after much discussion and debate to run four of the stories and to reject a story I wrote on Israeli censorship of the Arab press. They argued persuasively that the censorship piece did not fit the four articles which offered my personal observations on my trip to Palestine, the homeland of my parents.

(On each day that the articles were published and for several weeks after, the Chicago Sun-Times received criticism from some readers. It was a very difficult time, but the editors agreed the stories were balanced and offered a compelling and insightful narrative of life under Israeli occupation, a perspective that was certainly unique. It took courage on their part, not unexpected from Sun-Times management.

(The following year, the articles were nominated for a Pulitzer Prize. And although they did not win, they stand as a perspective that certainly is unique in this country.)

Israel Keeps Its Border Tight

(Originally published in the Chicago Sun-Times, Dec. 2, 1990, in a series titled "In Search of Palestine." Reprinted with permission, Chicago Sun-Times © 1996.)

Allenby Bridge, Occupied West Bank--The Israeli soldiers smile as they escort me to a special window in a cinder block building located on the border with Jordan, north of the Dead Sea near the ancient city of Jericho.

A Jordanian escort has dropped me off at a plank bridge spanning the Jordan River. The Israeli and Jordanian soldiers do not exchange greetings.

They are enemies, a point made clear by the imposing machine gun turrets that impose themselves over the checkpoint. Since Israel's creation in 1948, their two countries have engaged in war three times.

The Arabs call the span between the two lands simply *Jisr*. The Israelis call it Allenby, dedicated the British general who directed the Palestine Campaign in World War I.

There are two processing centers on the Israeli side of the bridge -- one for Arab residents of the West Bank and other Arab countries, and the other for tourists who, like me, carry U.S. or non-Arab passports. I have not seen the Arab center, but I was told it was dirty, crowded and hot. The tourist center is modern, with efficiency furniture and fans that circulate the hot, dry air.

But the Israelis are very alert, and they see that my name is different from that of other tourists who have entered Israel here and were quickly processed toward their destinations.

"Hanania? What kind of name is that?" a soldier asks from behind a bullet-proof glass window. He is comparing my passport to a security data base on his computer.

"It is a Hebrew word," I tell him. ``It means *God has been gracious.*"

"Ah, you mean *Chananiah?*" the soldier says with a broad smile that quickly disappears. He tries again. "Araby? What is your father's name?"

I know what he wants me to say. It seems like a game.

"My father's name was George." Very American-sounding I say to myself.

"What is your grandfather's name?" the soldier asks, having seen other Palestinian-Americans pass through this center on U.S. passports.

"Saba," I respond.

"Then you must wait over there."

The soldier points to a red plastic chair in a small waiting room where I sit for nearly two hours watching the other tourists walk through the exit door, seemingly unmolested.

Finally, two other Israeli soldiers walk into the waiting room. "Follow me, please," one says carrying a clipboard.

They are both young, maybe 20, with light brown hair, fair skin and blue eyes. Their khaki uniforms are loose fitting and their walk is casual. Each has a machine gun slung casually over his shoulder.

The first soldier tells me to step through a silver metal door.

"Now, please, take off all of your clothes. And empty all of your pockets. Give me everything that is written."

He doesn't answer when I politely ask why. It's not smart to protest too vigorously against a man who carries a machine gun.

I stand there naked before this soldier as he takes a cylindrical metal detector in his hand, and slowly runs it across every part of my body. When he nears my thighs, he takes the detector by the end and lifts it up against me and then looks up at me, expressionless.

"You think I have something under my skin?" I ask, still not angry but very embarrassed.

"You never know," he says.

I slowly put my clothes back on, black jockey shorts I bought from Marshall Fields in Chicago, an aqua polo shirt from The Gap, and Blue Jeans from the Orland Park shopping mall. My Nikes are in the bag that the soldiers have X-rayed in another room. My wallet, keys, coins and personal objects are scattered on a small wall shelf.

All that seems to meaningless at this moment. My future as a traveler in Israel and the West Bank is still uncertain as the soldiers huddle at the far end of the room, whispering in Hebrew.

Now I am scared.

My interrogator continues to probe, opening every note in my wallet and scrutinizing every photo, including one of my daughter. The soldier slowly and methodically flips through the pages of a travel book, *Israel: On Your Own,* and he orders me to count my money as he runs his fingers across the long hair on my head, as if he is looking for something.

"Where are you going?" he asks, continuing his search.

"I'm going to visit relatives in Jerusalem." That's not exactly true. Relatives I know from my mother's side are in Ramallah. My father's relatives whom I have never met, live in Jerusalem.

He nods and continues reading everything I own.

Outside the waiting room, the soldiers have already opened my black East Bank Club bag and placed it on a small counter next to my camera. My belongings are dissected slowly, separated on a shiny metal counter tat reminds me of an operating room.

A young woman soldier greets me. She is wearing sandals that show her unpolished toe nails. Her long blond hair is pulled back in a French braid. I try to guess her heritage. Maybe she is from the Netherlands or Russia. She's not an Arab.

"Please step up." She smiles and she starts to take the objects out of my bag, slowly. She hands me my camera and says, "Please, take a picture of the ceiling." every sentence begins with "please" now.

I understand some of this, I say to myself. Security is tight when two countries are at war.

But I have passed through security checks in many other cities, and this is different. In Amsterdam, where I pause to change planes during my trip, security guards also searched my belongings, and ``patted" me down. But they also did that to everyone who boarded the plane.

Today, I am honored by these soldiers because of my race. My heritage. Both of my parents are Palestinian. The Israelis did not stop any of the other passenger who accompanied me on the bus from Amman, Jordan.

I am still very scared.

There is no one left in the building. I turn the camera on, and point it at the ceiling as ordered. As I do, all of the Israelis step back to a far wall and I am left alone at the counter when I snap the shutter.

The female soldier now takes my hair dryer and plugs it into a nearby wall. She turns it on, feels the warm air, then turns it off.

The soldiers carefully feel through every inch of the clothes I have packed for this trip to the West Bank. As they finish, another female soldier carefully folds them--better than I had originally--and then puts them back into my bag.

"Here you are, Mr. Chananiah. I hope you have a nice trip," the woman says.

She hands me the bag, but as I walk to the jitney cab service that is designated to carry Arab visitors -- seven in a car -- I realize that I have left my dignity in little the room behind the large silver door.

West Bank Scarred by Bullets

(Originally published in the Chicago Sun-Times Dec. 3, 1990, in a series titled "In Search of Palestine." Reprinted with permission, Chicago Sun-Times © 1996.)

Ramallah, Occupied West Bank--I sit beneath the bullet-scarred bay window of a two-flat overlooking Main Street, where most of the bloodiest confrontations between Israeli soldiers and Palestinians have taken place on the West Bank.

There are eight bullet holes in the windows of this apartment where I have been welcomed for a short stay. Next door, they tell me, the windows of the home have five bullet holes. In the windows of the building across the street, there are six.

I learn that often when a bullet strikes a window pane, the glass does not shatter. Instead, the bullet leaves a small jagged hole before hitting the opposite wall.

"At first, we used to have the windows replaced," said Habib, 27, one of the family's three sons. ``But, now we just use tape to cover them up. We hope there will not be more."

But there always are.

This is a war zone.

On the deserted predawn street below, strewn with broken tear gas canisters, bullets broken glass and rocks, a convoy of heavily armed Israeli soldiers crawls past.

Large spotlights from their truck cut through the mist and flash against the metal accordion curtains that shopkeepers pull over their store entrances at night.

The soldiers are searching for signs of the *Shabab*, the young

Palestinian men who are fighting the *Intifada*, the Arabic word for the uprising against Israel's 23-year military occupation of the West Bank and Gaza Strip.

I see groups of youths, many in their early teens, huddling at nearby corners. They have made little piles of stones near each corner so they are ready for confrontations with the soldiers.

As the soldiers patrol, they scatter the stones with their feet or pick them up and toss them into a field. They break the glass bottles that are sometimes used to make Molotov cocktails.

At first, the crackling of gunfire is frightening. The soldiers fire their weapons into the air. I duck behind the wall under the windows, fearful that another bullet will sail through the living room. But my hosts, still seated upright on their chairs, tap me on the shoulder and smile.

``We don't worry about death here,'' says Marwan, who is about 26. ``We are all going to die. If you die, you die. Look at the window. How do you hide?''

The sound outside subsides and the morning stillness returns. This is the beginning of my three-day stay in the miserable battlefield called the West Bank.

Israel captured the West Bank and the Gaza Strip, two portions of land that once were part of a larger area called Palestine, in the Six-Day war against Syria, Egypt and Jordan. The former British mandate had been divided by the United Nations in 1947 into Arab and Jewish states -- really six disjointed sections of Arab and Jewish populations spread like wine stain over the map of the eastern Mediterranean. The Palestinian Arabs rejected the plan. The Jews did not.

Ramallah is near the geographic center of what would have been the heart of the Palestinian State. It is a city of about 200,000, one of the largest urban areas in the West Bank, with narrow streets lined by old brick homes and surrounded by farmland and hills. Relatives I know from my mother's side live here.

The morning begins with a spartan meal, mostly vegetables

grown in a three by six foot garden. They must keep the garden hidden, and they hope that the tomato and cucumber plants do not grow too large. If the Israelis find it, they explain, they will be fined 100 hundred Israeli shekels (about $50) because they do not have a license that's required to grow food for barter or sale.

This family of eight has encircled the garden with several cars to hide it from view. The cars, eaten through by rust, are no longer usable because the family cannot pay for a license, which costs nearly 500 shekels.

I dip thin, homemade Arabic bread in a dish of *dibbis*, a sweet mixture of crushed sesame seed sauce (*tahini*) and a liquidy marmalade made from crushed grapes taken from fields outside the city. It is sweet and very tasty. For me, it is like eating a peanut butter and jelly sandwich for breakfast.

Another dish contains olive oil and the crushed leaves of a bitter green Palestinian plant called *za'atar* mixed with sesame seeds.

"*Za'atar* is something that we must buy from the Israelis or grow clandestinely," another brother explains. "If the Israelis find that we are growing it, they can confiscate it. We must have a license to grow it, but the license costs several hundred Israeli shekels."

I sip thin, hot milk from a small glass and peer through the window nervously. The fighting has moved on, but minutes later, another squad of Israeli soldiers clutching M-16s, tear gas launchers and night sticks, beat on the door of the shop across the street.

Someone has painted a political slogan on the wall, and the owner of the building is ordered to come out and paint it over. If he refuses, he can be placed in detention for six months, or fined 350 shekels

The man comes out and, using white wash provided by the Israelis, drags a paintbrush across the Arabic letters.

From the distance I hear the popping of automatic weapons. And the soldiers in front of our building stand in readiness, expecting stone throwers to emerge from the dark passageways between the buildings.

Trying to ease my fears, I ask the family about their lives.

Fedwa, 17, hopes to be a teacher someday. She tells me that eight months ago she was walking down the street just before curfew (imposed periodically by the military authorities) when fighting broke out nearly a block from where she stood.

She turns her back toward me, and reaching downward lifts up the hem of her pant legs to expose her ankle. She points to where a ``rubber'' bullet struck her in the leg, shattering her ankle.

"Here is a `rubber' bullet," Marwan says.

I hold it in my hand, rolling it. It is cylindrical and very heavy.

``The Israelis used to use these rubber bullets," my hosts explain. "They shove them into long pipes they attached to the front of their rifles, when they are not using live ammunition."

"These are what they use now," he says. They are all over the street, along the curb gutters, in the yards and sometimes in the houses.

Look at this," he says. He has pried the plastic covering off the bullet to expose a half-inch metal ball bearing.

"This is a plastic bullet. If you are hit with this, you can die."

He gives me the souvenirs to take back to America.

When we leave the house for a walk in the streets of Ramallah, I learn that Palestinians are required to carry identification cards. Orange ones are for the West Bank residents. Green ones are for those that have been arrested in the past. The ID must be displayed on demand and it is demanded often.

"Sometimes they take our ID's just to give us trouble," Marwan explains. "If you don't have an ID card, you can be placed in jail. If they demand the card from me, I have to give it to them. And they can take it without reason at all."

As we walk down the street, an Israeli patrol suddenly orders us to stand against a wall.

A friend tells me not to be afraid. It is "normal."

We all put our hands up against a nearby store wall. My companions hand their identification to a soldier as another pats each of us down. My ID is a U.S. passport which the soldier inspects carefully. I can feel the barrel of the rifle in my back.

The soldier doesn't ask questions. My friends tell them I am related to a family that lives down the street. The soldier gives the passport back to me and they continue their patrol, entering a home they have taken over for the day to use as an observation post.

Palestinians are also required to display a different colored license plate on their cars. A number on a small white background tells the Israelis which city the driver is from.

Color coding makes it easy to tell the Palestinians from the Israelis, so the Israeli cars can easily be waved past the many roadblocks. Arab cars are always stopped and searched. On a one-hour drive from Ramallah to Jerusalem on this day, we are stopped three times to be searched by Israeli patrols.

I know that I have to muster a lot of strength to subdue my fears each time I stand in front of armed soldiers.

Tomorrow, my hosts tell me, they will introduce me to the young men and women who stand in front of the Israelis and hurl stones.

Uprising is Rooted in Hatred

*(Originally published in the Chicago Sun-Times Dec. 4, 1990,
in a series titled "In Search of Palestine." Reprinted with
permission, Chicago Sun-Times © 1996.)*

Ramallah, West Bank--``We hate the Israelis. And the Israelis hate us."

It was a precise summation of how badly relations have deteriorated between the Arabs and the Israelis in the three years of the *Intifada*, the Palestinian uprising in the West Bank and Gaza Strip.

Issa, the son of a family I am spending several nights with, sits on the tattered couch, an *Oud* held tightly in his lap. The *Oud* is a stringed Arab instrument usually heard playing sprightly melodies in cafes and lounges.

But this night, Issa is plucking the notes of Palestinian revolutionary songs banned by the Israelis. His songs are emotional and they come from experience.

Last year, Issa, in his late 20s, was arrested by the Israelis and placed at a detention camp in the Negev Desert called Ansar 3. It is an open air facility, heavily guarded and surrounded by razor wire and fencing.

No one has escaped from Ansar 3.

"It is called the camp of slow death," Issa says.

"I was accused of leading the *Intifada*." He laughs and then continues. "Everyone is leading the *Intifada* in this city. Everyone. But they said I was a terrorist, and they put me in the prison for six months. When I got out they ordered me to sign a statement in Hebrew, confessing to my crime. There is no proof except what you sign, so I refused."

His mother sits at his side, proud of his musical abilities and also of his prowess as a leader of the *Intifada*.

He no longer smiles as he continues his story.

"After they released me from Ansar 3, the harassed me each night at my home," he says. "One day, they came in the middle of the night and grabbed me."

"They took me into the mountain and the soldiers said I would die. They beat me with sticks and a rubber hose, across my face and my body and they ordered me to sign a confession. Finally, they lifted me up; my hands were tied behind my back. There was an argument in Hebrew. One soldier wanted the officer to stop. But he pulled out a gun and put it against my forehead."

Issa's mother starts to cry as her son demonstrates with his hand.

"I was afraid. I could do nothing. I would not sign. The soldier stared into my eyes and he smiled."

"I closed my eyes and I remember hearing the trigger snap and the gun explode in my face. I jumped with fear. The sound was like thunder against my ears and I saw the flash."

He lived because the gun was filled with blanks.

Issa spent four months in bed at home until he recovered from the shock. But to all gathered this night, he is a hero.

``Every day there are beatings," says Suheil, who has been assigned to escort me around the city. He often helps reporters, when they are allowed to enter the occupied zone.

Israeli soldiers often bar reporters from entering towns in the West Bank and Suheil tells me not to identify myself as a reporter, because I could be expelled. Jet black hair and eyes, his face is hardened and shows little emotion.

"We are fighting a war," Suheil says as he leads me through alleyways and darkened streets of Ramallah.

As we walk, Suheil lifts his arm and makes me stop. "Look

down the street," he says.

I see nothing.

"There they are."

I look harder and see the barrel of a guns sticking out from behind a building.

"We will see another patrol soon. They send them here as bait, to get us to throw stones and then to run. They hope that we will run into their trap. But we see them."

A younger man, about 17, who already has been stopped, says something to Suheil as he continues to walk away.

"He says there is another patrol hiding among the buildings that we have seen. We always try to help each other."

I am concerned now, because I wonder if they plan to throw rocks at the soldiers.

But Suheil says, "We are just watching. Just watching."

In the distance, a young man climbs a telephone pole and ties a Palestinian flag to the top. He climbs halfway down, then jumps and starts running, and the soldiers start their chase. Displaying the Palestinian flag is outlawed by the Israeli occupation authorities.

Suheil takes me back through the gangways of houses until we return to the home of my hosts.

Together, we huddle in the front room listening to the Israeli soldiers firing their weapons, and wonder whether any of the Palestinians have been shot.

The next morning, the flag is removed and life is back to normal.

Did the Israelis capture anyone, I ask?

"When they do, they always yell `Bingo." It means they have found someone," one of the boys says.

"When we hit an Israeli soldier with a stone, we yell Bingo back!"

No one yelled Bingo last night in Ramallah, I am told.

My father was born in Jerusalem, and I ask my friends to take me to the house. It was on Jaffa Road, just outside the new city of Jerusalem.

But the road has been changed since 1948 when the Israelis took over, and the homes have been modified. We search for an hour and fail to find the house.

My mother was born in Bethlehem, which has been in Israeli hands for only 23 years.

My father, George Hanania, arrived in America in the 1920s, went to school at DePaul University and then joined the U.S. Army, serving in the Middle East. After war broke out in Palestine and Israel was established, his family fled Jerusalem and stayed at a refugee camp in Jordan until my father and another brother helped bring them to Chicago.

He married my mother in 1952 and brought her to Chicago's South Side where I was born. I have been told about their homes and their lives all my life. But this is my first trip to see the land and the family for myself. I speak just enough Arabic and my relatives speak just enough English so that we can understand each other.

But it is clear from the conditions of their lives that they are not happy.

We find the old stone home of my mother's family intact on Medbussa Street in the town revered as the birthplace of Jesus.

The Arab family that now lives in the building understands, and they allow us to walk into their home so I can see the small rooms, curved archways and the tiled floor, much of it the same the day my mother and father were married in 1952.

In a corner is an old tree planted by my grandmother, Regina. My aunt is reflective as she says, "We have moved many times since the war, but this old tree will always remain. Our mother told us that one day in the future we would look at this tree and remember her and our lives. Today, we look at this tree and we remember why we are here, refusing to leave."

The worst stories are about families whose homes have been destroyed. In Ramallah, there have been too many to count, my hosts contend.

"The Israelis don't even need proof. They only need a suspicion that someone in the household is involved in throwing rocks or fighting the soldiers," one of my escorts explains.

They drove me past a home that was destroyed by the Israelis. A large five-room house now stood like a pile of rocks, shattered by bulldozers. The family apparently had fled to the home of relatives in another village.

As we stood there looking at the home, one of the young Palestinian escorts remarked, "All they have done is given us more stones to throw."

Mother Cuts in on Soldier's Pursuit

(Originally published by the Chicago Sun-Times Dec. 4, 1990.
Reprinted with permission, Chicago Sun-Times © 1996.)

Issa's mother is very proud of her sons and the other young boys who live on her block. She is loved in return. In fact, she is called "the mother of Main Street."

Her long black hair hangs over one shoulder, tied back by a small wrap that she made at her home. Her dark brown eyes show the strain of three years of war.

The boys gathered around her now tell of the day soldiers chased a dozen of them to her doorway.

"I opened it and rushed the boys into the kitchen, where we all grabbed chairs and lined them up," she says, a small triumphant smile forming on her lips.

"When the soldiers came in, they asked why all these kids were in the kitchen. I had a scissors in my hands," she says. "I was cutting their hair."

The Land is All -- to Two Peoples

*(Originally published in the Chicago Sun-Times Dec. 5, 1990,
in a series titled "In Search of Palestine." Reprinted with
permission, Chicago Sun-Times © 1996.)*

Sharafat, Occupied West Bank--The rolling hills are green and covered with olive trees, their twisted branches sagging with heavy fruit as such trees have for more than 2,000 years.

It is a land, in Palestine, that my mother and father often spoke about to me: a rambling field of olive trees and small orange groves on the northern border of Jerusalem, west of the Arab Village called Dheir Tantour.

To Palestinians, the land is everything, symbolized in the red, white, green and black of the Palestinian flag.

The ownership documents are filed away in vaults in the Office of the Ministry of the Interior in Jerusalem, a building my relatives have visited more than two dozen times since 1970 when two-thirds of Sharafat was confiscated by Keren Kayemeth, the agency that owns land that will remain ``forever" the property of Israel's Jews.

According to those documents, the land belongs to my grandmother's nephew who now lives in Colombia with his family. They fled Palestine after the 1948 Arab-Israeli war and the land was maintained by my aunt.

After Israel captured the West Bank and Gaza Strip in 1967, the government approved several laws that made land owned by absentee owners subject to special provisions. Those provisions allowed the government to confiscate the land and use it for Jewish settlements.

Much of Sharafat has been renamed Kibbutz Gilo. The a cluster of modern homes and apartments built for Jewish settlers and immigrants to Israel hugs a hillside, glimmering in bright sunshine. Non-Jews are prohibited from living in the kibbutz, and sometimes they are banned from working the land.

Israel has confiscated thousands of acres of land that belonged to Palestinian Arabs both in Israel and in the occupied West Bank and Gaza Strip, angering the owners and feeding the already deep animosity both peoples have for each other.

My aunt lives nearby in Ramallah. She explains that much of the anguish felt by Palestinians comes from the loss of their land, and that I could not understand the feelings until I saw the land and felt the dirt in my hands.

"That is what life is all about," she explains.

Friends take me by car to Sharafat and Kibbutz Gilo, a short journey from Jerusalem. But our car is prohibited from entering the kibbutz.

Settlers at the gate anxiously inspect my passport, recognize that I am a Palestinian and promptly turn us away.

"Look at how beautiful the land is," my driver says as we slowly pull away.

"We used to have a small house there that we rented to a man who helped harvest the trees. The house has been destroyed. They also destroyed the two wells that were on the land."

Pictures of the structure are not impressive. The building was far from accommodating than the ultra-modern kibbutz apartments that cover one of the hillsides overlooking the former Arab farmland.

"They called this land Esther now," the driver says forlornly.

"We still call it Sharafat -- even though what we have left are the rocks and what they have are the olive trees and the beautiful gardens and the lovely hills."

My driver is very emotional, and her eyes well up with tears.

"When I first went to the ministry and said that I wanted to file a formal complaint against Keren Kayemeth, they all laughed at me," she says.

"The man said to me, `Old woman--are you strong enough to fight the government? All alone? By yourself?' I said `Yes, as long as I am strong enough to live."

The maps kept by the government now designate Sharafat with red lines and warnings in Hebrew that say "Don't Cross."

"Every year we would rent out the land," my driver says.

"Every year we would pick the olives from it and sell them. Every year the land helped keep us alive. Every year I represented our cousin, who is afraid to come back to Palestine. Frightened by the Israelis," she says scornful of her cousin whose name is still on the deed to the land.

She feels that he, too, should come back and fight to regain the land, although the sturdy kibbutz buildings make that nearly impossible.

"We want our land back," she pleads.

I can only offer her sympathy as we continue on our journey.

To Israelis, the land is also important: it is biblical Promised Land paid for in the blood of the Holocaust.

But that does not concern Palestinians of the West Bank who now spend their days farming small plots behind their homes.

On one plot of land near my aunt's house, there is no room to plant an olive tree.

But the small farming oasis boasts a flourishing garden with tall vegetables held on a stick and broken wood fences.

The rim of a tire serves as a pot for a tomato plant.

"It is not Sharafat, but this small piece of land will help us to survive," says the garden's owner.

Nearby, another family has converted a broken refrigerator into a pigeon coop.

"This is how we make money," the owner explains, pointing to his two dozen pigeons. "I raise them and then sell them. People like them as pets, and sometimes they eat them."

Five years ago, this 34-year-old man lived in the United States, working as a laborer in Chicago. He proudly displays his US residency card, although he says he has no plans to return with his American wife and three children.

"I could leave here at any time, but I won't because this is my home. Maybe someday when the war is over, I will go to the United States when I can be proud of what is being done. But today, I see all of these people and how they live and I cannot go home."

The man's brother also raises birds. In the evenings, he painstakingly builds wood and wire cages for the canaries that he and other family members catch in fields outside the village. He has several dozen canaries in cages that hang all over the home.

"People (Arab residents of the West Bank) pay a lot for these canaries," he says proudly. The yellow, red and green birds chirp happily away, it seems.

"People like the way they sound, the songs they sing. I think they are signing songs of freedom."

Not everyone buys them. Some people see them as bad luck and would rather they be freed.

In a lot across the street from their home, other families have erected small stands where they sell fruits and vegetables and pigeons and canaries that they, too, have raised in their homes and backyards.

There are also crates of olives and dates. When money is scarce, because jobs are few, they will barter for a specific reason.

"We have to do whatever we can do to prevent from paying taxes," says a villager.

As I end my three-day stay in the West Bank, I am glad to leave. Hardship is everywhere. The years of trouble in this land have scarred both sides. Each day brings new reports of killings. The victims are Arabs and Israelis.

If I wanted to find a glimmer of hope that there will be a peaceful settlement to the decades-long battle, I did not find it in the villages of the West Bank or in the Jewish sector of Jerusalem.

But what I did find was a determination on both sides, including among my relatives, to survive and to maintain their heritage.

Two peoples laying claim to the same piece of land. I crushed in my hand a clod of dirt from the garden behind one of the Palestinian homes. As it fell from my fingers, I tried to understand.

I'm Glad I Look Like a Terrorist

I'm glad I look like a terrorist.

Tall, dark, swarthy complexion. Longer-than-average black hair. If you didn't like me, you might say I have ominous looking slits for eyes and little brown fingers with that natural "trigger finger" look.

It's not a common look -- and not something to really brag about.

But sometimes, it does come in handy, like last week, when I was returning from a two-week vacation visiting cousins in South America.

The "look" prompted several floating customs officers at Miami International Airport to abruptly, but politely, yank me from my spot in a line as I waited impatiently with some 50 other travelers to pass through customs.

At first, they just scrutinized me from nearby.

The sweat was dripping down my temples -- I was wearing a wool suit for my return to Chicago's arctic weather. I had one camera hanging from my left shoulder, another one on my right, a bag in each hand and a third that I nudged across the tile floor as the line of returning tourists inched forward.

I had been in line 20 minutes when the customs men finally came up to me and asked to see my passport. Then they told me to follow them. And they weren't about to help me with my bags.

"Where have you been?" one asked.

"Venezuela," I said, panting from the 30-yard jaunt from the line to the small office where they conducted the "interrogation."

"Any other countries?" the other asked.

"No." They must not have believed me, because they asked that question three more times.

"Put your bags up on the counter and open them all," he said.

That's when the horror struck me. My God! They were going to discover that I was a tourist trap junky!

Squirreled away in my luggage, between the underwear and baggy white pants, were six sets of maracas, five water gourds, four wood carvings, three hand carved flutes, four hand-painted coconuts carved into faces and -- gulp! -- six stuffed crocodile heads fashioned into leather openers. All cheap trash.

The maracas wouldn't stop rattling when the big bag splashed open.

After slipping their fingers into every nook and cranny, tapping the inside walls of the luggage and lifting up piles of old socks, one of the government men asked, "Do you have any drugs in here?"

Do people ever answer "Yes" to that, I thought?

After about 20 minutes of squeezing and poking around, the agent finally turned to me and asked, "By the way, what do you do?"

"Oh ... ahem! ... I'm a reporter for the Chicago *Sun-Times*."

Everything stopped and they closed my bags.

"Well sir, everything looks fine. Thank you for your time. Goodbye." The agents rushed off, and a skycap walked up to load my bags.

"What was that all about?" I asked.

"Oh, terrorists -- drug smugglers. You know. You have that special look."

Eying all the people who were still waiting in line, I said with a smile, "That's fine with me."

(Reporter Ray Hanania, really a nice, all American guy, usually only terrorizes subjects of his Page 10 Column reports.)

(Originally published in the Chicago Sun-Times, Feb. 24, 1986. Reprinted with permission, Chicago Sun-Times © 1996.)

Miss Liberty

Zaki was leaning to one side of his cab as he waited impatiently for the light to change.

The last thing on his mind was "Miss Liberty" and the 100th Anniversary celebrations planned across the United States for the Statue of Liberty.

He was more concerned with earning a living.

But somehow, the subject always seems to come up when I am in a cab.

"You an Arab?" he asked as he gunned the car through the intersection.

"Yeah," I said "How did you know?"

"Your face," he said.

"You speak Arabic?" he asked again.

"*Nifta* (a little)," I replied in Arabic.

"*Shu ishmick?*? (What's your name?),"" he asked in Arabic to test me further.

When I told him, he curled an eyebrow and asked, "What kind of name is `Ray'?"

The conversation started on the standard route. First, we talked about the Middle East wars, Israel and the Arabs. Then we exchanged sympathies for the Palestinians. Then we talked about anti-Arab bias and how foreigners have it rough in the United States.

"One couple got in my cab the other day, found out I was an Arab and wanted to get another cab," he said. "They portray us as big-nosed, camel drivers wearing robes and a *hattah* (turban). Nobody cares."

Well, not quite, I interrupted. We portray ourselves. I started telling him about my dad, and let loose with an "How to be successful American" lecture. It was a lecture I learned from my father.

George Hanania left the "old country" in 1923 with the help of the British Mandate government in Palestine and the Jerusalem Post Office, where he and several other relatives worked.

He was impressed by Miss Liberty. He learned English, found a job at the Astor Street Theater, then the Rolling Green Country Club, and became a citizen as soon as it was legally possible. And, when World War II began, he joined the US Army and the O.S.S. serving in Europe.

My dad wanted to be an American. That meant understanding how the system worked and doing things the way Americans did.

He never forgot his heritage; he just left it in his suitcases and family albums.

Of course, certain things take time to change.

When he got back from overseas duty, he went back to the "Old Country" to find a bride. His family introduced him to my mother, Georgette. She was 20 and he was 45 at the time. He saw her one day carrying a water jug through Manger Square in Bethlehem where she lived. They were married within four weeks.

The first thing they did in the United States was to visit Miss Liberty.

He told her that Miss Liberty was a reminder that everyone in this country was an immigrant like her and that when they stepped upon this soil, many of them couldn't speak English either.

And Miss Liberty, he said, was a guarantee that they would have the opportunity for an equal chance at living a happy and free life in America.

That was the key word. "Opportunity."

Although Miss Liberty opened the door of opportunity to my parents, it was up to them to find their way around.

And they tried. Mom spent the first five years here learning English with a Greek woman, Esther, who lived next door.

That's when I arrived on the scene. When I was born, they gave me what they thought was an American name. And dad gave me these words of advice.

"Don't ever forget that you are an Arab," dad would say. "But always remember that you are an American first."

Why, I asked?

"Because when Americans look at you, they are looking to find something familiar, to see if you are like them. If they see that you are like them, they will listen to you and sympathize with you. But if they think they are looking at a man who is a foreigner, whose allegiance is really, deep down, to another culture or country or ideology, they will fight you no matter how right your arguments are."

I tried to explain all that to Zaki, who had pulled up at the curb to drop me off.

"Here you are, Mr. American," he said with a smile.

I smiled and shut the door after I paid him.

It won't do any good, I thought to myself.

But he has found something in America he won't find in most other countries.

That's the freedom to live anyway you want.

(Ray Hanania, who writes for Page 10, plans to spend his July 4th weekend visiting with immigrants -- at a family picnic.)

(Originally published in the Chicago Sun-Times on July 4, 1986, and originally titled "From Immigrant Dad, a Lesson in Liberty." Reprinted with permission, Chicago Sun-Times © 1996.)

It's Always A Polaroid

It isn't that it's so insulting to be mistaken for a terrorist.

It's that it is insulting for the "terrorists" I am mistaken for.

I am probably one of the only tourists who carries his passport in his breast pocket when I drive past an airport.

Every time I set foot in one, the agents come out of the woodwork and give me the "Third World Degree."

Airport porters have reminders posted near their terminals that refer to the profile."

"All commuters that meet the profile must be checked in inside."

See, I understand being stopped every time in Miami, Chicago and New York airports.

I fit that profile.

I look like a terrorist, at least the kind that we always see on television and at the movies.

It's the people that they mistake me for that usually hurts.

And it's always a Polaroid picture that's shoved in my face as evidence, the "cause" for the inconvenience of stopping me and pulling me aside at an airport.

I was strolling through Miami International Airport with a companion, from the Air Mexico terminal to the baggage claim when I noticed that eight men all wearing the same light grey colored "Members Only" jackets were positioned in pairs, forming a near octagon around us. They all had their hands tucked into their jacket pockets and, more suspiciously, they weren't looking at me directly. At least, that's how it seemed. I could "feel" their glances, though.

When we paused, they paused.

As we started, they started. It was almost funny.

How do they decide when to swoop in, I don't know, but they did and after all of them turned to face us, one of them stepped forward and asked me for identification.

They didn't ask "Can we see your drivers license." They always asked for a passport first.

What terrorist wouldn't have a passport?

"Who are you?"

"Airport security, sir. Can I see your ID?"

"Sure. What did I do?"

"Are you returning from a trip?"

"Yea. Cozumel. Ever been there?"

I dug my hands into my shirt pocket and he asked me to place the black carry-on bag on the tile floor. I did.

"Here." I handed him the passport.

Two other men walked up and escorted my friend a few steps away.

"Are you with him?" they asked her. Maybe they thought I kidnaped her. I don't know. But they weren't taking any chances.

"Where're you going?"

"Chicago," I said with a sigh. "Listen. This happens to me all the time. I look Middle Eastern because I *am* Middle Eastern. American ... Arab. That's it. I served in the US Air Force, active duty during the Vietnam war, and my dad served in the OSS during World War II. I even served eight years in the Illinois Air National Guard. And," ... and this usually ended the hassle. "I'm a reporter in Chicago. For the Chicago *Sun-Times.*"

The agents made a few calls on their walkie talkies and the one that confronted me walked back up and handed me my passport and bag.

"Sorry for the inconvenience. It's just routine."

Sure it was, I thought. It's always routine for me. "But what was that picture you were holding?"

The agent responded, "We thought you were someone else.

You're name Carlos?"

Real funny, I thought. "Can I see it anyway?"

The agent held it up in front of my face. Not being rude, just matter-of-factly.

"That guy is ugly. He's at least 30 years older than me. That guy doesn't even look like me."

The agent pulled the Polaroid away and they returned to their prowl.

But if it were the only time, I might not have thought anything about it.

After returning from the Middle East in 1991, airport security yanked me out of line before I could even set foot in New York's Kennedy Airport. I had just stepped off the plane and was walking through a long, mirrored passageway. Right away, I knew I was in trouble when I looked at it.

Sure, it's there for the convenience of the passengers.

"Can you come with me, sir?" This time the agent was a little more cocky and apprehensive.

"What's up?" I asked with that not-again feeling.

"Can we see some identification?" he insisted.

"Sure."

I started to dig deep into my carry on bag and two other agents walked up behind me.

"Careful, please," the agent warned me.

"Here we go again."

"You get stopped before, Mr. Han-ya-han-ya-na?" the agent asked, reading my passport.

"Ha-na-KNEE-Ya," I responded. "Frequently. I know. I know, I look like some terrorist suspect on a picture you got."

The agent pulled out a color Polaroid snapshot and looked at it and looked at me. He passed it around to his colleagues, all of them wearing jackets.

I'm convinced they use the pictures as a prop. Can't be the real guy. A great excuse when you have to apologize, or explain the stop away to innocent passengers.

"Can I see that?" I said handing him my Chicago *Sun-Times* identification as he folded the passport shut.

"A reporter?" he asked.

He turned and talked to another agent and handed me the passport and newspaper ID back.

"Thanks sir. Sorry for the inconvenience."

"I know, but can I see the Polaroid?"

The agent handed it to me again. It was different from the one in Miami. This guy was not only ugly and older, but he was wearing a baby blue leisure suit from the 60s and a white Panama hat. And he was looking right at the camera. Smiling. Maybe a smirk.

He looked more like a reject from *Saturday Night Fever*, rather than a terrorist from the movie *Black Sunday*.

Now, I didn't doubt that this guy in the Polaroid was a terrorist suspect. He was looking right at the camera. The only thing he brandished was a smile.

But I had only one question for the agent before they sent me on my way.

"How the heck do you get a terrorist to stand still and pose for a Polaroid picture? You guys must be pretty good."

An Electoral Lesson

What made me place my name on an election ballot in March 1992, I don't really know.

But I did know that if I wanted to become a political consultant advising candidates on how they could improve their campaigns, I would have to experience the process firsthand.

While several Arabs of Lebanese ancestry, most second and third generation, have reached the heights of the American political system, few Palestinians or "real" Arab American activists have joined their ranks.

American politics is not about "strangers," it is about "friends."

Friends are people you know. Friends are people you identify with. Friends are people you vote for.

I discovered the hard way, as a candidate with a distinctly Arab and Palestinian name, and despite more than 17 years of public celebrity as a reporter, I was still a "stranger" to most voters.

I ran for two offices, as a delegate in the presidential elections, and later as a candidate for the Illinois General Assembly.

I didn't expect to win either race, although I was determined to give it a real effort. But I didn't expect my ethnicity to be as big of a factor as it turned out to be.

I really thought that all those hundreds of appearances on the various TV panel programs, the thousands of radio programs I hosted, and the hundreds of articles and columns I wrote for the Chicago *Sun-Times* and the *Daily Southtown Economist* newspapers would help me overcome any disadvantages I might suffer because I was Arab American.

As I discovered, being Arab American has distinct disadvantages. The further I distanced myself, the weaker those disadvantages would be. The closer I was, the stronger they were.

And I was close.

I wanted to be close.

I wanted to be the first Palestinian American elected to the US Congress, not to represent Palestine, but to show the nation that Palestinian and Arab Americans were in fact *real* Americans, that we *are* concerned about this country, and that we are reliable partners in making it great.

Running for office is difficult enough without going into it with a perceived ethnic "handicap."

The primary races for presidential delegates in March 1992 seemed the most likely place to begin my initiation.

I examined my assets, and one of them was that I had served in the US Air Force *during* the Vietnam war.

Although I did not serve in Vietnam, when I enlisted, I didn't know that President Nixon was about to end the war.

The field of presidential candidates included Arkansas Governor Bill Clinton, who looked like a longshot back then, New York's Gov. Mario Cuomo, the 300 pound gorilla of the Democratic party leadership, and Nebraska Senator Robert Kerrey.

It was Kerrey who attracted my attention. Kerrey was a Vietnam veteran who won the US Congressional medal of Honor. And, he was being described in the media as a "nascent dove on Iraq," which meant to me that he might be strong enough to support an evenhanded approach on Middle East subjects.

I called his campaign coordinator in Chicago, who was heading the Illinois campaign, and asked to be considered as a delegate.

At first, he was enthusiastic, especially knowing my background as a reporter and my name recognition. I may have been controversial, but I was always very high profile.

Several days later, after conferring with his staff, he called to tell me that the national campaign advisers believed my Arab heritage would be a disadvantage and therefore they could not consider me. Kerrey was a Kennedy-esque candidate and it was, after all, a

Palestinian who murdered Senator Robert F. Kennedy in 1968. And, it was implied, Kerrey was trying to avoid criticism that he was "soft" on Iraq.

At first I didn't believe it. I wanted to fight back. I wanted to prove to them that I was an asset. And then I thought, what good would that do?

I re-examined the presidential candidates and concluded that if my ethnicity was going to matter, it should matter in a positive way to someone who was perceived as an ethnic candidate. I walked into the headquarters of the Cuomo for President Committee, a committee that had not yet been sanctioned by the candidate himself, but that clearly had forced Cuomo to leave the door open.

Phil Krone, a political consultant whom I had known as a City Hall reporter, headed the committee and he welcomed my delegate candidacy. His staff helped prepare the documents I needed to place my name on the ballot, but getting the signatures of registered voters on my nomination forms was all up to me.

And I ended up doing it alone, standing outside the local Dominicks and Jewel Osco soliciting passers-by for their signatures.

It was cold in the middle of the winter. My hands were shaking, and I averaged about 10 signatures an hour. I needed something like 300 signatures, I think. I don't remember the exact number, but I recall that several people would smile, ask what I was running for, nod in support when I said Cuomo, and then ask me what my ethnicity was as they signed my petition.

Politics is personal. And in Chicago, even in the suburbs, nothing is more personal than ethnicity.

Irish candidates, unknown to the world outside of their neighborhoods, can easily win elections to the highest offices. Names like Sheehan, Kelly, and Flanagan were powerful vote magnets for unknowns who had only limited public and political experience. It didn't matter whether it was for local legislator or Cook County judge. They beat out incumbents with more ethnic and less Irish names.

Hanania certainly would not be mistaken for an Irish name. It was Hebrew. If you removed the "H," it could become Italian. If you saw me, I could be Hispanic. If you heard me, I might be Greek. But definitely, not Irish.

My loss had nothing to do with my ethnicity, that election. I ran third behind two other Cuomo delegates in my district. We all ran in fourth place, as a team, losing because Cuomo had refused to enter the presidential race.

Clinton and Kerrey were the heavyweights. Clinton won.

Apparently, I didn't do that bad, because the local Democratic leaders in the congressional district approached me after the primary and asked if I would consider filling a ballot vacancy and running for the Illinois Legislature as a Democrat.

No Democrat had run in the Democratic primary, mainly because the Republican incumbent was a veteran floor leader, State Rep. Larry Wennlund, and considered unbeatable.

This time, because I was being slated to fill a ballot vacancy in the November election, I didn't have to stand on street corners and beg voters for their signatures. Instead, the party leaders from the district voted to endorse me, and they submitted my paperwork to the Election Board in Springfield, Illinois. My name was on the ballot.

Right away, though, Wennlund tried to knock me off.

I hadn't even raised a nickel yet, and already Democratic Party lawyers were spending thousands to keep me from being removed.

Although the local Democrats endorsed me, I didn't get much help from the state Democratic leadership, guaranteeing my loss.

I had covered hundreds of election campaigns as a reporter and I knew exactly what I had to do this early in the campaign: I had to raise money.

By the end of the campaign, I had raised about $65,000. More than 90 percent of the money had come from Arab Americans in Illinois, mostly from outside the district, and several from around the country. Popular radio DJ Casey Kasem, an Arab American, had donated $200.

Leaders of several Arab American organizations pledged to raise as much as $30,000. They managed to raise about $15,000, which helped, but most of the money came from one-on-one meetings I had wealthy Arab American businessmen and families whom I had to convince that my candidacy had a purpose.

I told them I expected to win. We all wanted to believe that. After all, who would support a candidate who expected to lose?

But the overriding factor in their support was that my candidacy would help to give the Arab American community direct experience in the electoral process.

In other words, I really didn't have to win to be a winner if my candidacy could help galvanize the Arab American community and raise their involvement in this very important American process.

And that was the message I was trying to make to my community. You don't have to win to be a winner!

We couldn't rightly claim to be Arab Americans if we didn't get actively involved in politics.

It's not enough to talk about it.

We had to register to vote.

A rough census of the district where I ran showed that there were some 4,000 Arab American surnamed families, which could be equated to about 10,000 real votes. Most Arab American families averaged about 5 people -- two and one-half people, on average, were of voter age in each family. Unfortunately, I could count the number of registered Arab voters in my district on one hand.

I had to reach out to the non-Arab voters, which I did.

Wennlund wasn't stupid. After all, he was in the leadership of the Republican Party in Illinois and had won election three times before. An attorney, he had more than enough money to produce slick, multi-colored, glossy direct mail brochures, the kind that I would have produced had I the money.

Most of his $150,000 plus campaign fund came from riverboat casino interests that he helped push through the legislature, or from clients of his law firm.

He paid for at least six mailings to the district's 45,000 voters. That cost money, about 32 cents per piece, which meant that it probably cost him about $90,000 to direct mail to the voters.

I spent $8,000 on two mailings, limited by budget, to about 15,000 voters. Two colors. Black and white pictures. They were designed to help remind the voters of who I was.

Ironically, my biggest problem was the news media. They ignored me. Charges that I had made during my campaign were not reported during my campaign, but became center stage two years later when Wennlund was challenged by another Democrat.

But I did manage to make the inside cover of *Time* Magazine with a quote that a *Tribune* reporter thought was funny and gave to them. The media wasn't interested in issues. They wanted "news." So, when Wennlund refused to debate me, I gave the media what it wanted.

The campaign had been pretty dirty as we rounded the corner to the final weeks. Wennlund supporters were picketing businesses owned by my relatives and friends. Angry at some of the charges, I facetiously offered to settle the election in a Park District boxing ring. And, I noted, that not only did Wennlund have a lousy record as a legislator, but he was a "lousy dresser, too!"

Of course, most voters were more interested in the presidential campaign.

Bill Clinton, a southern governor awash in scandal, had won the Democratic Party nomination. Despite some highly publicized scandals, he was within threatening range of Republican incumbent President George Bush, whom most Arabs supported.

The way Arab Americans viewed politics, Democrats were liberal and more supportive of Israel and the Jewish community. The Republicans supported Israel too, but placed a higher priority on wealth and Middle East oil.

But Bush had led the nation in a war, earlier in the same year, against one of the most hated foreign dictators of our time, Iraq's

President Saddam Hussein.

It probably wasn't the best time for a Palestinian Arab to pick to run for public office, especially when anti-Iraq hysteria was reaching record levels each week during the campaign.

I did get a lot of support from Jewish leaders, many of whom recognized me as a fair and reasoned Arab community activist. And on election night, I did very well. But, not well enough.

The 38th Legislative District is divided between two counties, Cook, which is heavily Democratic and urban, and Will, which is heavily Republican and Wennlund's base.

Even if an Arab did well in the heavy Jewish voting blocks in Cook County, there was no way that a farmer was going to vote for that "Ay-rab."

And, someone in Larry Wennlund's campaign wanted to make sure that message didn't escape those Will County farmers.

In the final week before the election, a letter was mailed to residents of Will County, signed only by a "concerned citizen," and denouncing me as a "foreigner."

"Mr. Hanania is a well known anti-American activist who has supported Arab terrorist leaders including the PLO's Yasser Arafat and Iraq's Saddam Hussein. He says he is Palestinian, but we know that he is *really* Iraqi."

There was little I could do that late in the campaign. I was lucky enough, as it was, to have enough money to pay for two mailings and 8 billboards touting my candidacy.

While I carried Cook County with a very slight margin, including the predominantly Jewish districts, Wennlund killed me in the Will County farmlands, defeating me more than 26,000 to 19,000 district-wide.

Some might have looked at the election as a landslide loss.

But I looked at it as a victory.

I had received more votes than George Bush averaged in 88 of Illinois' 102 counties. And, I reckoned, my vote totals were among the highest of most Arab Americans who currently held office.

My vote totals followed the percentage of the vote totals of the presidential candidates in my district. I had received nearly the same vote total as the typical Democrat running in my district, while Wennlund had received the average Republican voter turnout.

In my district race, I did better than Clinton, who lost votes to Independent Ross Perot.

Had this been some other district, and some other race, I might have won.

I turned around and formed a political consulting firm, and using my experiences as a candidate, worked with some 40 candidates for elective office.

Initially, the prospects were encouraging.

Only two candidates hired me and then fired me because I was a Palestinian. One was a Jewish candidate for judicial office whose husband felt my presence on the campaign would injure her election.

On the other hand, a Chicago alderman who was Jewish and had a large Jewish voting constituency kept me as his campaign manager and consultant even though some in his campaign believed I might also bring harm.

Alderman Bernie Stone won re-election with a heavy margin and his head upright.

The Miracle of
St. George Church

What is a miracle?

Is it the event? Or is it the impact an event has on the people who experience it?

At St. George Antiochian Church in Cicero, the pastor there is contemplating that very thought as he witnesses a stream of tens of thousands of people who are traveling from all over the world to see, firsthand, an Icon of the Virgin Mary that on April 22 began to tear from both eyes.

St. George Church, opened in 1965, happens to be an Arab American church. Most of the parishioners come from the Middle East. Many of them were actually born in Bethlehem, the site of some of the world's greatest Miracles.

On April 22 of this year (1995), the pastor of the church, The Very Rev. Nicholas Dahdal, had arrived to celebrate the Liturgy for St. Lazarus Saturday and the Feast of St. George. It was a special occasion for the church and its parish because the church is dedicated in honor of the night that St. George was martyred. It was the end of lent and the beginning of the Holy Week.

You can hear it in Pastor Dahdal's own words:

"I had invited a Catholic Priest, Father Douglas Wyper, to celebrate the Liturgy with me. While he was entering the church, he noticed a spark, or some kind of a shine on the Icon of the Virgin Mary. I was called out by him to come and look. And I saw two streaks coming down the eyes of the Virgin Mary. As we watched, another two streaks came down."

Father Dahdal immediately called Bishop Job of the Orthodox

Church of America, in Oak Park. Approximately a half hour later, Bishop Job arrived at the church to see the Icon for himself. He immediately knelt down in front of the Icon and began to pray.

"That same night, I contacted my archdiocese," Father Dahdal recalled.

"And his Grace Bishop Basile came down the following Monday, April 25. When His Grace arrived in front of the Church, he started to cry, before he even saw the Icon. I asked him why. He said he didn't know but he saw something special. He came into the church and he saw the icon, investigated behind the Icon and he went out and did a prayer service, called Akathist."

That night, the Bishop contacted Church Officials in New York.

"The following Monday, May 3, Metropolitan Philip Saliba arrived with Bishop Antoun, another auxiliary. When they arrived, he had absolutely no doubt that this was the greatest thing that he had ever seen in the 28 years of being an archbishop. Immediately, that evening, he declared it a miracle, and he gave it a name. He called it the Miraculous Lady of Cicero Illinois. And the church was declared a Shrine of Our Lady."

I asked Father Dahdal what has happened in the weeks that have followed the miracle.

"People are coming from all over the world to see the Icon. We have had people come from the Philippines, from Holland, from Lexington Kentucky, from San Francisco California. This morning we had two ladies from Chile South America. I had people come from Florida. A bus arrived from Detroit, from Indiana, from Iowa," Father Dahdal said.

"I have a magazine from Poland with a full page cover of the Icon on it. We have a newspaper from Mexico with a front page story and picture of the Icon. People have heard this message around the world.

"I even received a letter from a prisoner in West Virginia, letters from people all over the country. I see a tremendous impact on the people who come here. They leave with such satisfaction. We have

Dad standing with his family in their Jerusalem home, from one of our earliest photographs taken around 1920.

Mom posing at the Bethlehem studios of Michel J. Basil, around 1946.

Mom, standing center, with her family in Bethlehem, just before her marriage in 1952.

No. 48971

H/1499

GOVERNMENT OF PALESTINE

PROVISIONAL CERTIFICATE

OF

PALESTINIAN NATIONALITY

LAISSEZ—PASSER

Valid until the 31st December, 1926

The bearer ......GEORGE HANNA HANANIA.......

......A PALESTINIAN.......

whose photograph is attached and who is described below has been
granted this document to enable him to travel abroad and return to
Palestine

Date 10th August, 1926.

for A/ *Controller of Permits*

........Jerusalem........

Dad's laissez passer (Palestinian national identification certificate), issued in
1926 just before coming to Chicago to meet his brother and to study.

Mom outside the hospital with newborn Raymond, April 1953.

Mom poses in Arab garb with my brother John next to our silver Christmas tree.

With my Godmother, Minnie Stiff, in front of our real Christmas tree, 1957.

At my high school prom.

Theta Chi fraternity photograph, Northern Illinois University, 1973

Just out of Air Force basic training, December, 1973.

Editor and Publisher of
The Middle Eastern Voice
Newspaper, 1976

Posing on a camel while touring
Morocco for the Middle Eastern
Voice Newspaper, 1976.

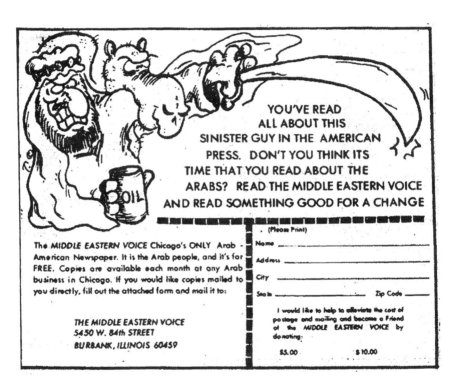

YOU'VE READ ALL ABOUT THIS SINISTER GUY IN THE AMERICAN PRESS. DON'T YOU THINK ITS TIME THAT YOU READ ABOUT THE ARABS? READ THE MIDDLE EASTERN VOICE AND READ SOMETHING GOOD FOR A CHANGE

The *MIDDLE EASTERN VOICE* Chicago's ONLY Arab - American Newspaper. It is the Arab people, and it's for FREE. Copies are available each month at any Arab business in Chicago. If you would like copies mailed to you directly, fill out the attached form and mail it to:

**THE MIDDLE EASTERN VOICE
5450 W. 84th STREET
BURBANK, ILLINOIS 60459**

. (Please Print)

Name _____

Address _____

City _____

State _____ Zip Code _____

I would like to help to alleviate the cost of postage and mailing and become a Friend of the *MIDDLE EASTERN VOICE* by donating:

$5.00 $10.00

Subscription form for The Middle Eastern Voice Newspaper.

Southtown reporter Ray Hanania and Sun-Times reporter Harry Golden, Jr., at Chicago's City Hall, 1980.

Addressing the Chicago Chapter of the American Arab Anti-Discrimination Committee (ADC) Convention on "Media Awarness".

God answered my prayers in 1985, and I was hired as a Chicago Sun-Times reporter. Me standing in front of one of the Sun-Times trucks promoting my Page Ten Column.

(Photo By Rich Hein and the Chicago Sun-Times. Reprinted with permission, Chicago Sun-Times © 1996)

Frontrow seat as a Chicago Sun - Times City Hall reporter covering a press conference with Chicago Mayor Harold Washington in 1986.

Receiving an ADC media award in 1988 from Chicago Mayor Eugene Sawyer, with Palestinian businessman Talat Othman (left) and Palestinian activist and friend, Fadi Zanayed (right).

miraculous cures taking place at the church. There was one woman who came to the church several days ago for an incurable disease that she had. Four days later, she came back and said that it was gone," Father Dahdal said.

"There was a woman who came to the church who came to the oil mixed with the tears and anointed someone with a growth on their neck, and that person was released from the hospital and the tumor has been reduced tremendously."

No one can say whether or not the miracles have taken place ... if you only think of it as an event.

But Father Dahdal points out that the event itself is far outweighed by the faith of the people, which is just as important.

"Last week, a young man who was dressed in a street gang member's leather jacket, with street gang symbols and signs, came to the church. He stood in front of the Icon and stared at it for 10 minutes. The next thing I saw, he was on his knees for 20 minutes crying. He got up, took off his street gang jacket, and left it on the floor as he walked out.

"These are the small little miracles that change people's lives.

"How has it affected our lives?" Father Dahdal said in answer to my query.

"It has turned our lives upside down, but in a good way. It has brought many people to the church, many people who have never been here and many people who were here before. It also opened the eyes of many people to the church, especially those who didn't know there was an Arabic church."

It even affected the Pastor.

"For me, it changed my own outlook. I had a very negative outlook on American life because of the problems of broken families and troubles that we see. There is so much crime, and uncaring, and hurt in the world around us. But since this has occurred, I have come to see so many people and to learn to feel for them. It has brought many people together and it has brought us together especially as a church."

In today's day and age, that alone is a small miracle.

Christian Arabs are very close to their churches.

And religion, traditionally, is the venue for Arab educations.

My mother was educated at a school run by French missionaries in Bethlehem. Even many Muslims attended schools run by Christian evangelists.

Generally, though, my family is Orthodox Christian.

When they came here, to the United States, though, there were very few Orthodox Churches. But being very religious, they had to find a church. Oftentimes, if there was a Greek Orthodox Church, they would attend there.

My father had been married previously. His first wife, Walbert Mueller, had died giving birth to my brother. On Christmas Eve.

It's a tragic story, although the impact on my brother was not that harsh.

He was raised at a Lutheran Home, for several years, placed their on recommendation of his mother's family, later spending summers with foster parents and relatives in Wisconsin.

When my dad remarried, and he tried to put his family back together, we enrolled at a Baptist Church on Chicago's far south side.

I recall my mother saying how much she liked to watch the Baptists when they prayed. There was so much emotion. Demands for salvation. The whole upbringing under evangelists was something that remained in my mother's blood for years. And she took me with to a Billy Graham Revival at the old McCormick Place downtown. I remember mom walking up to the podium with me in tow, "accepting Jesus" and confessing her sins in public.

In our early teens, my Uncle Assad convinced my mom to enroll us at a Lutheran Church near our home, where he and my Aunt Lillian later got married.

We went through confirmation as Lutherans and attended the Lutheran Church services as kids, although mom and dad started attending a new "Arab" church that had opened up someone near

Oak Park. (This was the same church that later relocated to a new church building in Cicero as St. George Orthodox Church.)

The truth was, my parents disliked the American Christian churches, even though they were very religiously inclined. The dislike stemmed from the politics. And it was most evident during Christian holidays like Christmas and Easter. So while my parents let us attend Lutheran Church services during non-holidays, they took us to the Orthodox Church during major holidays where we didn't have to hear about how Israel was fighting to survive and the Arabs were bringing on the Armageddon.

At every pulpit, whether it was the Baptist Church, the Lutheran Church or the Catholic Church, which was the closest to my parents Orthodox religion, the pastors, priests and deacons constantly spoke about "Israel" and God's promise to the Jews.

Ironically, these Christian pastors were not being pro-Jewish. The bottom line, to them, was that the Jews would not go to heaven, although their plight as the "Chosen people" would bring about the final Armageddon.

That was a sensitive topic in our home, because God's promise to the Jews was the euphemism that Zionists exploited among American Christians to justify their colonialism and conquest of Palestine during the early part of the 20th Century.

Although I wasn't an Arab "activist" at a young age, and my ethnic pride was still "stored," whenever we sang Hymnals at Bethany Lutheran Church at the top of the hill on Jeffery Avenue near Pill Hill, I always mumbled when it came to the word "Israel."

I wasn't anti-Semitic. I wasn't anti-Jewish. Some of my friends at the Church *were* anti-Semitic and were constantly criticizing me for hanging around with "Jews." They were my friends. But deep down, still unnurtured, I understood a primal urge to mumble through passages about Israel when we sang our Christian songs in Church.

It was odd. Even during Confirmation classes at the Church, which brought me together with some of the toughest "greasers" in my school, I would shrug off notions about God's promise to the

Jews, and I spent much of my time with Jewish friends. Yet, the greasers in the class who hated the Jews so much, and constantly bragged about going out and beating up Jews, absorbed the teachings without so much as a whine.

That is the essence of American anti-Semitism.

Most Americans hate Jews, but accept the biblical teachings about Jews as a part of their basic religious upbringings.

Arabs, who really did not hate Jews as a race, ethnicity or religion, were stereotyped as natural enemies of the Jews because of the political orientation of the American country.

Criticism of Jews by Arabs was more of a defensive act, while the hatred that many Americans had toward Jews came from pure anti-Semitism and racism.

And while Christians and Muslim Arabs really distrusted each other, carefully hiding their own prejudices, non-Arabs viewed them all the same. In fact, the typical American couldn't tell the difference between a Christian Arab or a Muslim Arab, or between a Jordanian, Syrian or a Palestinian. In fact, we were often confused with Iranians. This American hatred was also tied to American current events. During the Hostage Crisis in 1979 and 1980, American hostility toward Arabs stemmed from their hatred of Iranians, Muslims and anything Middle Eastern.

St. George Orthodox Church was an oasis where these problems were rarely discussed and the pastor there spent most of his time trying to balance the rival agendas of the Christian Jordanians and the Christian Palestinians who each vied for control of the parish coffers.

The crying Icon of the Virgin Mary brought them together and reminded everyone that there was something greater than individual pride, hatred or lust.

And at least for a moment, it brought non-Arabs to the Church by the thousands.

Sunrise in Jerusalem

My body and eyes are awake, but my mind is still sleeping, drained by the 24 hour journey and jet lag from Chicago. It is just before 4 in the morning and from my second floor window at the Mount of Olives Hotel, I can see the beginning as night gives way to day, a cyclical reminder of the mystical powers that exist beyond man's realm.

Next door to my hotel, a green compact Fiat with yellow Israeli license plates pulls up to the driveway shared by the Mount of Olives Chapel of the Ascension and an unimposing Mosque with a five story minaret tower. They tell me that as natural as Islam was to follow in the footsteps of Christianity, so too were the early decisions by Muslims to establish Mosques at nearly every Church site or Christian religious landmark.

Considered a part of the Old City or Arab section of Jerusalem, beyond the ancient walls to the East, the Mount of Olives is mentioned several times in the Old Testament. The octagonal Chapel of the Ascension covers the rock where Christians believe Jesus ascended to Heaven. And around it is the Garden of Gethsemane and the tomb of the Virgin Mary.

From dawn until evening, Christian pilgrims wander in an out of this holy area, but they are careful to avoid the Mount of Olives Hotel, which is Palestinian owned and frowned upon by the Israeli Government Tourist Office because it caters to Palestinian politics and Arab delegations, many of whom critical of Israeli Government policies.

The owner of the small Fiat, wearing a large white Muslim turbin and street clothes, walks up the seven broad cement steps to the Mosque entrance.

The minaret of the mosque has four loud speakers wrapped around its tip, each held in place by tall green pipes. Around the top under the stone crown are a row of colored bulbs, blue, red, yellow, white and orange.

And every morning at 4 a.m., or thereabout, the call to the religious faithful echoes from the speakers of every Muslim Minaret throughout the Holy Land, including the one perched directly above my hotel window.

"Allaaaaaaaaah uuuuuh Akhbaaaaaaaar!" The Islamic prayer begins.

The call of the Muazzem, most likely from a tape recorder, sounds more like a yell, breaking the silence that drapes Jerusalem.

To Muslims everywhere, it is their signal of prayer obedience and one of five times each day that they face Mecca to confirm their faith in Mohammed and God.

To non-Muslims in this politically charged area, and especially to the Jews who claim Jerusalem like some glittering jewel, it is an unwanted reminder that this holiest of holy cities is under contention.

Signs of modern man contrast the great historic significance of this site. The roof of the two-story Chapel of the Ascension is flat. On it, a homemade solar plate with a tall, aluminum tank, provides the electrical currents needed to heat the building's water. White bed sheets, shirts and other laundry clothes-pinned to a nylon rope flutter in the wind, seemingly in pace with the morning church chimes that follow the call to prayer.

A cacophony of roosters, birds and car engines slowly gather momentum. And, within an hour, the pre-dawn blue, red and grey sky comes to life above the city's skies, awakening the City of Jerusalem. By 5:40 a.m., the sun's rise in the East slowly begins to caress each and every Jerusalem building, moving from the tips of the highest sky-scrapers downward as if exposing the city scape's brilliance.

From the window of my hotel at the Mount of Olives, a modest

Arab-owned establishment full of Palestinian pride but few modern amenities, I can see the entire city, hugging several small hills that appear to role from North to South with the panorama below.

Two things immediately stand out from Jerusalem's landscape as the sun makes it's way upward from the East: The Dome of the Rock is clearly the centerpiece of Jerusalem. It is the closest structure in my view and it's large golden dome appears to be the largest structural object in Jerusalem's still Biblical panorama.

The golden dome radiates above the city's more mundane building colors in unavoidable contrast. The Mosque structure itself is a deep blue and black stone color, sitting furthest East in the ancient Old City of Jerusalem. The wall that encircles Jerusalem's Old City are hugged on the eastern slopes by tombs and cemetery stones. Next to the golden dome, one can clearly see the empty, white cement courtyard and arches.

The second most noticeable figures in Jerusalem's landscape are the towering buildings that are rising on the north and on the west, outside the Old City's walls in New Jerusalem, which became populated during the turn of the century.

These 15 or so story buildings rise from the top of the hill that the city embraces, and you can count from the left eight tall buildings, and eight smaller buildings of 10 stories or less.

Between these two epicenters of the city's profile rest the small, beige, single and double story homes of the old quarter, separated by clumps of lush green trees and rising evergreens.

Every house and building is distinct in the morning light. It seems as if you can almost count them all individually. The city seems so small, like an engineer's miniature rendition of work yet to be done.

Israeli settlements surround this once proud Arab city, and it is today impossible to see where Jerusalem begins and where it ends. It no longer looks like the weathered city map that was the walled centerpiece of my father's office that I grew up to know.

In front of me, below my window and across the street, quietly sits a dirty old camel, tied to the white metal fence that surrounds the Garden of Gethsemane. Flags of blue and white and white crosses marking the era of Constantine flutter in the wind above. The camel is relaxed on its haunches, legs folded underneath its large body. It's head is nestled in a cardboard carton where the owner has placed some food the night before. It hasn't made a noise, but its long neck allows it to peer above the box and a single hump of patchy brown that will carry its elaborate saddle to comfort the inquisitive tourists.

It turns its head in reaction to the loud cawing of the large ravens that perch nearby and whose sounds replace the Muazzem. These birds appear to be saddled too. Their dark black wings each have a small white diamond at the elbow, and cover the bird's light brown body.

The back of the camel's head has a beautiful dark brown swatch of short fur, crisscrossed by the leather bridle that wraps its face and mouth. Each time the camel dips its head into the box and snatches some food, it pulls it out and begins the slow process of chewing. His head moves side to side. His large lips make a steady mulch and satisfied grin. Underneath his swaggering chin is another large tuft of beige hair.

The camel sits in a small dirt and stone field next to the road and behind a small Arab-owned restaurant called the Tent. His grunts are distinct and he begins to catch the eye of tourists and others as cars and trucks begin to pass by, their engines straining to come up the steep road.

Not to be left out of the city's life, the bells of the Christian Churches start to clang from different quarters of the city. The cool breeze that sets these sounds will, later in the day, turn into a needed relief to the scorching day's heat.

There is very little manmade noise outside, although you can occasionally hear the distinct engine grind of a large truck making its way up the hilly, winding Jerusalem streets.

What a way to wake up in the morning.

I'm Glad I Look Like a Terrorist

A Midsummer's Night Dream

I *dreamed I was in a Hollywood Movie ...*
I dreamed that I stood at the crest of a great hill overlooking the world. On a white stallion draped in silk and gold.

On my head, I wore a blue turbin, a scimitar in my hand, held high above my head.

The history of the world was but a nightmare. In my dream, I saw the future of war and conquest, the spoils and the fruit.

Salah'adin was but a warrior, and I was his king.

My greatest conquest lay before me. Palestine. The heart of the fertile crescent. The center of the known world. The origin of the Great Religion and its one, true God, *Allah.*

In my dream, there was no mandate.

In my dream, the armies of the West did not exist, and the war of the worlds were still fought in the sands.

My bravado was a greater weapon than the steel and iron bullets of the future. My courage was a greater bond. My vision was the greater mandate.

There was honor in confronting your opponent face to face.

In His eyes, Muhammad realized the conquest of billions of people on a planet that was defined in sand.

And in his wisdom, Jesus suffered, a prophet not just of God but of conquest.

Moses and Abraham were my fathers. They stood in my shadows with Jesus and Muhammad at their side.

The sound of the Ram's horn was a call to the faithful, and a chariot of greater glory.

My steed sailed across the waves of a great ocean of sand,

leading a horde of the faithful. Faith was the great momentum of success. The sound of its wings breathing life into the people, singing a song of gathering that formed the community.

I could see beyond the oasis. A glow from the conquest ahead. The razor sharp blades of our scimitars slashed through the wind, separating the fearless from those who feared.

Triumph reigned like the jewel in a crown.

A simple life comforted the victory. We sat around a large platter filled with spiced lamb and rice. A fire crackled in the fore.

Over the horizon we watched as the sky turned deep blue, a red fire embraced it below.

There was no fear of the infidel.

Our families were safe.

Our land was secure.

Our future was determined.

Our faith held us together.

There was nothing to be needed. Nothing to be imposed. Nothing to be harmed.

Under the stars so bright. A million stars. A million eyes celebrating the Celestine aroma of an Arabian Night.

We could not see the hordes of civilization coming. Industrialization meant nothing.

We did not see the threat.

Behind the thin veil, time appeared to be our friend.

The sleeping giant that protected the people died at the hands of time.

And we sat helplessly exposed. Awed by the New World's technology. Naive to its ways. Married to the strong traditions of a weak reality.

Infirmed in the world. Captive to our traditions.

We lost the great battle that we could only now see in our dreams.

I'm Glad I Look Like a Terrorist

The Arabian Diaspora

A *l-Nakba* -- the catastrophe -- is the Arabic phrase for the great tragedy of Palestine in 1948.

It is the equivalent of *Shoah*, the Hebrew word for Holocaust.

To the Palestinians, *al-Nakba* was *Shoah*.

We were the victims of perception and propaganda, things we did not understand as a community.

One day, Western technology drove into our country under the army of a military victory.

The next day, strangers from new lands arrived at our shores settling in areas we cursed, using Western technologies to achieve miracles with the land.

By 1948, Palestinians saw their world erupt into disaster.

Where would they go?

By 1948, my father had already immigrated to the United States with the help of another brother, Mousa, who worked at Rolling Green Country Club.

They had been in the states for years, and dad had found work at the Astor Theater downtown as an usher. He lived with a cousin and aunt on the near north side of Chicago, on Clyborn Avenue near an old brewery.

When the war broke out, his brothers and mother had fled Palestine and ended up briefly in a refugee camp under Jordanian control.

With my dad's help, they came to Chicago, where everyone pitched in to purchase a home.

This was the first war of dispersion.

Palestinians from throughout Palestine had fled the war, fearful of the onslaught and reports of Jewish terrorism against civilians. Stories about Deir Yassin were rampant, and the shadow of people like Menachem Begin and Yitzhak Shamir, leaders of notorious Jewish terrorist organizations, hung over the refugees as they sought refuge with relatives or the shelter of tent camps administered by the United Nations.

Education and religion had something to do with how the people fled.

The majority of the country people were Muslim.

Few of them had relatives in other countries.

They ended up in refugee camps and they stayed there for most of all their lives. Generations rose and fell in these camps as war after war scarred Palestine and changed the landscape of their homeland forever.

Their dream of a land long gone no longer matched the reality, which they were unable to actually ever see.

Those who lived in the cities and who were educated found refuge and support among families that had already sought new lives in foreign lands.

These Palestinians were mostly Christian, back in 1948, educated in Western missionary schools in Western thought and in English.

Many educated Muslims also followed too. But the bulk of their people remained back home in the camps.

While my father's family found direction in America, arriving in New York's Ellis Island and migrating to Chicago where my father had already started a new life with his brother and cousins, my mother's family remained in that part of Palestine which had not yet been occupied by the Israelis and had been taken over by the Jordanians.

They lived in Bethlehem, and in the late 50s, finding no work in the harshly administered West Bank, they fled to South America where hundreds of thousands of other Palestinians had sought refuge too.

They also settled in South America and in the Caribbean islands

I'm Glad I Look Like a Terrorist

of Jamaica and Honduras.

Cities with obscure names like Maracay in Venezuela, Baranquilla in Colombia, and Cochabomba in Bolivia.

Arabs looked very much like Hispanics and South Americans. They blended in easily. They quickly learned Spanish. They immediately set up businesses, creating major Arab warrens in these sweltering South American cities.

By the late 60s, they had factories and retail stores dotting the South American horizons.

In Macaray, the second largest city in Venezuela, they had joined up with dozens of other Palestinian and Arab families. Canahuatis. Handels. Marzoukas. Taruds. Dabdoubs. Kronfils.

In Maracay, my *Siede* Saba owned two stores. One sold shoes. The other sold suit cases. They lived upstairs above their stores, opening at 6 in the morning and closing at 8 each night.

Sunday was the only day that they remained closed.

Outside, South American life continued, almost unaware of the growth of the Arabs in their communities.

I remember standing on a hill in Caracas, the capitol of Venezuela, with an Uncle who had traveled there to sell wholesale clothes and supplies to an international distributor.

From where we stood, you could see the city's skylight. Buildings that rose into the sky. Maybe 15 or 20 stories at most, towering over the nearby homes, but were easily reduced to speckles by the mountains that surrounded the city and rambled through its neighborhoods.

My uncle pointed to each building on the horizon, and surprised me when he said, "That one there is owned by a Palestinian. That one there is owned by a Jordanian. That one there is owned by another Palestinian. That one there is owned by a Jew."

In the early 60s, the Arabs arrived in these foreign lands and by the 70s, they were playing major roles in local politics, wielding their money and helping these countries develop their oil industries. In fact, many of them rose to political power themselves, as presidents and prime ministers in Jamaica and also in Argentina.

In Kingston, Jamaica, Arabs there dominated the downtown retail stores, sharing commercial strips with the Jews.

We fought against them in Palestine, but shared with them prosperity in these foreign lands as neighbors.

We ate at the same restaurants. And we even did business together, buying and selling each others' wares.

Business made our families strong, strong enough to allow us to dream about our Palestine.

Although I could never find my father's home in Palestine, I always found family homes in many foreign countries. I could travel anywhere and be welcome.

We were all over the world.

The populations didn't seem to mind us until the late 70s, when the Palestinian Revolution had found its momentum, and terrorism was making an international statement.

The massacre at the Olympics, the hijackings and even the hostage-taking at Entebbe airport, impacted this dispersed community tremendously.

It became hard to travel.

It became hard to live.

Visits to Maracay that had been so enjoyable in the 60s as a child with my parents, had turned into terror in the 70s.

One evening, two Venezuelans had tried to break into my Siede Saba's electronics store, the new one they had opened only a few years earlier to sell Casio recorders, watches and other electronic novelties.

When my uncles ran outside with shotguns and pinned the men down on the street, a crowd of Venezuelans gathered around yelling in Spanish, "Go home you Syrians."

They called all the Arabs *Syrians*, whether they were Palestinian, Jordanian or Lebanese.

The crowd started to get ugly and my Uncle Fawzi was forced to let the two thieves go under the protection of the crowd that continued to grow in size. Their angry voices getting louder. Their fists raised in the air.

I knew very little Spanish, but I could easily recognize the hatred and the anger in their voices and in their eyes.

We weren't just people whom they disagreed with. We were foreigners raping their lands.

Why did we have stores in *their* country?

Why didn't we go home?

Why didn't we go back to Palestine? And leave Venezuela to the Venezuelans.

I could understand all that through the yelling and the cursing.

My uncle's shotgun was now pointed at the crowd, and our family slowly filed back in under the iron gate that had been lifted just enough to open the front of the store.

Even when the Maracay police arrived, backed up by Venezuelan soldiers, they told us we should go inside and keep our mouths shut.

We were welcomed as strangers. But once we became Arabs, we were told to leave.

It didn't matter how many buildings my uncle had pointed to on the horizon.

It was clear that we were forever foreigners in a foreign land.

No One Met Me on Jaffa Road

Once I realized I was an Arab, I wanted to know everything about my family.

Naturally, I started with my father.

I looked for his passport.

But he had none.

Dad died in 1970, when I had just turned 17 years old.

I really didn't know him. I never got to ask him about what it was like to live in Palestine.

All I had were some suitcases of photographs to explain where I had come from.

The pictures were detailed, but they were empty too.

They said very little. Black and white. The edges were trimmed in the 50s style, like a postage stamp.

The black and white had begun to turn a faded brown. Even the notations in ink on the back identifying each scene was written in Arabic.

Dad didn't want me to speak Arabic, but he left me a legacy in a language I had to struggle to understand, had difficulty speaking, and couldn't read at all.

I knew he was born on Jaffa Road, just outside of the Jaffa Gate in Jerusalem.

He lived with his father, Mousa, and his mother, Katrina, who lived to a ripe old age of 82. *Sittee* (grandmother) Katrina lived with my Uncle Khamis and his family. *Sittee* Katrina had long black hair that was graying slowly. Strands of white hair mingled with the natural black hair that I was told reached down to her waist.

She didn't want it cut. Instead, it was rolled in a ball on her head.

Sittee Katrina could only speak Arabic. There were very few words we could exchange. I never did get to hear her own story, although I know that she was related to a family of prominent Palestinians, including one who participated in the United Nation's debate defending the rights of the Palestinians in 1946 and 1947.

I really wanted to know *Sittee* Katrina.

She always smiled at me and called me "*Habibi*" when we would come to visit.

But that was it.

Among the pictures dad left was one photo of *Seide* (grandfather) Hanna sitting in their frontroom of their house, surrounded by my *Sittee*, Uncles and Aunts. In traditional Arab culture, *Siede* Hanna held up a photograph of another Uncle, Mousa Hanna, who had already left for the United States. Taking the picture of the picture symbolized how much they missed him.

One more picture showed my dad on a staircase with his sisters and brothers. It was on the side of their home.

But no one could tell me where that was.

There was no address for the Hanania household.

The postman who knew where the family lived had long gone.

I walked up Jaffa Road on foot starting from within the city's walls.

But everything looked so new.

Jaffa Road was now a Jewish street. Romema was just a dream.

I walked up to several homes and just stared.

What would I ask the families who lived in the homes now? "Had you ever heard of the Hanania family? Did you know George Hanna Hanania?"

I could only stand on the cement walkway and stare at each house wondering if I was even close?

I thought about those stories I had seen on television about Jewish families who had returned to Poland, looking for their roots.

American television had thoroughly documented these stories of personal tragedy and journeys.

Their homes were not destroyed.

Despite the horrors of the holocaust, they still had buildings they could return to and find.

They still had doors that they could knock on. And the families that now lived there, felt remorse for their visitors, whom they had always expected to return.

They were welcomed and the meetings were cordial.

No one reached out to caress my pain. The sun was warm. The sidewalk was hot.

I wanted to knock on one of the doors and have the same conversation.

It was redeeming, it seemed, for the Jews who went back to their homes, and the families who greeted them.

I wanted that same feeling.

But the animosity was thick. You could feel it in the dark eyes that stared as I walked slowly up the street in the sweltering heat of the sun.

I wasn't threatening, but you could still sense that they were afraid.

But no one met me on Jaffa Road.

I stood there alone.

The Terrorist Threat in America Today

Talk radio is often called the "pulse" of America. And in the aftermath of the Oklahoma bombing, the pulse rate was high and tempers were angrily focussing on "Middle Easterners," Muslims and Arabs as the "terrorist" perpetrators.

After all, as one talk show racist in Chicago exclaimed before going to a break, "Who else would commit such a cowardly act?"

Well, regardless of the fact that no one really knows who committed the crime -- or that the ethnicity of the criminals may even soon be disclosed -- American hatred was quickly circling in on the "typical terrorists," the Arab.

Now, rationally, the ethnicity of the terrorist doesn't really mean much, except to explain some motives. Beyond that, the need to place an ethnic or religious face on the terrorist is meaningless.

But even before we even knew what the terrorists looked like, believed in, or what they wore, the country was already striking back in racist fashion against the usual target.

In Chicago, windows of cars parked in front of an Arab Community center were smashed. Arab women draped in religious garb where heckled and derided by American passers-by. The threats were subtle on radio and on television, but more direct and ominous in real life in streets across the country where Arab-Americans, other dark-skinned ethnics, and Muslims were present.

It started on Wednesday morning and continued through Thursday, until the FBI released a composite drawing of the two men wanted in the attack.

And, guess what?

Were they Arab?

No.

Were they Muslim?

Unlikely.

Were they "typical American?"

Yes.

Very "typical American" is how they looked to me. Ominous looking rednecks, one with a marine-type crew-cut, the other with threatening dark curls. (And those with dark curly hair are the most cutthroat!)

They both had that "typical American" thuggish look.

I found myself crying in front of the TV set, as images of dead bodies were dragged from the rubbled building. And I soon found myself screaming into the TV: We have to crack down on the terrorist threat of those murderous, fanatic, "typical Americans."

I couldn't believe myself, doing to them what they had been doing to us during the entire ordeal.

How else could I explain the inhumane murder of babies, children and innocent civilians, except at the hands of fundamentalist, extremist "typical American" terrorists.

Oh, how they fit the profile of killers, too.

Imagine, the greatest act of terrorism in this country committed by the threatening "typical American" terrorist.

What a horrible people those "typical Americans" must be. Animals. Murderous. Blood lusting monsters.

I had to rethink all the calls for legislation, including banning the funding of any "typical American" organizations, or prohibiting the immigration into this country of "typical Americans."

It was the only way to put a real end to "typical American" terrorism, a scourge on humanity that had reach new heights of horror in this country.

Is no Arab, Muslim, Pakistani, Indian or other Third World

ethnic safe anymore in this country?

America is supposed to be a place where we, the untypical Americans, can find refuge.

But once again, from the deep recesses of the darkest hole of terror comes this atrocious, despicable act of -- how did the President describe it during his numerous press conferences? -- "Cowardly."

That's it, this cowardly act of "typical American" terrorism.

I wanted to call the radio stations, too, and let off steam, expressing my own anguish and frustration at this despicable act of "typical American" terrorism. I wanted to tell the radio talk show hosts how much I fear going to the neighborhood shopping mall, bumping into these "typical Americans."

After what they did, how could I hold any pity for them?

Imagine how I felt as I listened to "typical Americans" try to "explain away" the brutality of this act ... "they did it to us and no one cared, so why is everyone so angry when we do it?" Selfish, I grumbled.

And, it happened in the "heartland" of, as NBC's morning host declared with emphasis on national TV, an area that has a concentration of "Middle Easterners."

Those poor Middle Easterners. How could they suffer through living with these "typical American" terrorist conspiring amongst their midst?

Isn't anything sacred anymore to hardworking Americans like myself, a Palestinian - Arab - American - Christian - single - parent with one child?

Could a person like myself with black hair, dark eyes and olive skin be safe in this country any more with the threat of "typical Americans" buying up our stores, entering our colleges, moving money from MY country to other "typical American" activities ... and, Oh my God, marrying our daughters?

Yes, the FBI should crack down immediately on the activities of "typical Americans."

The "typical American" Omnibus Terrorism Act should be approved immediately!

Because, you know how these "typical Americans" are.

This type of activity is, well, stereotypical of their beliefs. They are willing to sacrifice themselves and all they have in order to preserve the values of their "typical American" discrimination.

If the "typical American" terrorist can strike at the heart of an innocent "Middle Easterner" hamlet like Oklahoma City, is nothing sacred in this country anymore?

Now ... it is possible that the terrorist might turn out to be Middle Easterners, after all.

But, would it really change anything?

(Originally distributed on the Internet, April 20, 1995.)

Lessons of the Oklahoma Bombing

Amidst the rubbled Murrah Federal building and the victims of the Oklahoma City bombing is a lesson that must not be lost or swept under the carpet.

That lesson has to do with the respect that this country must "re-learn" about itself.

America is a nation of immigrants.

No one immigrant community has any greater right of "patriotism" over another.

Yet, we saw two different feelings expressed in the wake of this great American tragedy.

In the aftermath of the bombing, blame was directed at individuals described as "Middle Eastern."

This premature conclusion is not in and of itself wrong. Jumping to conclusions is the American way.

But what was wrong, and what did cause great harm to many Americans who are of Middle Eastern heritage, is that this premature conclusion became the basis of an emotional, national frenzy to retaliate. The anger was carried mainly by talk radio stations, although it was also used as a rallying cry by many otherwise well intentioned politicians. Some radio talk show hosts were both obnoxious and irresponsible in their attacks against Middle Easterners, Arab Americans and Muslims.

The pillage continued in the local newspapers.

One famous Chicago syndicated newspaper columnist even went so far to urge that we immediately pick a "likely" target (meaning a Middle Eastern nation) and bomb them.

I felt that is exactly what many in this country had already done. They selected an ethnic community, and bombed us.

As an Arab American my anxiety was great, not just because of the horror that I shared with the rest of the nation for such a horrible act of wanton murder, but because many of my friends began to look at me with suspicion.

As an Arab American, I was not involved in the bombing.

I do not support the use of violence to achieve political ends.

I oppose terrorists and terrorist organizations, and I support the peace process.

I repeated this each and every time I was confronted with tempered anger from my non-Arab American friends.

I felt shame as I listened to radio talk show hosts attack the terrorists and blame people of my heritage with being responsible.

Every time a radio talk show host called for retaliation against "foreigners" or "Arab countries" I cringed with fear knowing that I, my family and my relatives and my people would be the ones to suffer.

Every time a news report was broadcast about this terrible tragedy, my shame increased as the fingers seemed to point in a chorus of responsibility towards me.

The feelings suddenly came to an abrupt halt only days later as word began to spread that the suspects were in fact "home grown" terrorists, from places in this country like Michigan, Nebraska, Wisconsin and Texas.

My anxiety did not turn into anger against people in those states. I did not do what others did and urged that we immediately punish the people of those states for supporting extremist militant militia organizations, or right-wing extremists, or talk radio conservatives who support many of the goals of these militias.

Instead, I saw that America had reached a point in xenophobic finger pointing that might well serve as a lesson for all of us.

And that lesson is simple.

Terrorism, crimes of all sorts, and racism, do not have an ethnic face.

Terrorism does not go by a particular surname.

And it does not cloth itself with the symbol of any religion.

Terrorism is a crime with no face, no country of origin, no religion, no accent, and no skin color.

Let's all bow our heads together, as one people, and condemn this crime for what it is, not for what some would want it to be.

(Distributed on the Internet, December 1995.)

Speeches on the Arab Experience

Introduction to the Speeches

As hard as I struggled to be an "American," my Arab heritage always tugged at my soul.

It was not surprising that immediately after dropping out of college and leaving the Air Force early at the end of the Vietnam War with an Honorable Discharge, I found myself among the top of Chicago's Arab American community leadership.

I had what the community needed in 1975, arriving two years after the first Arab-Israeli war in which the Arabs had at least temporarily "won."

My Arabic was poor. But I had the ability to look, sound and act "American."

I was immediately named "spokesman" for the Arab American Congress for Palestine, Chicago's largest And most active Arab American organization.

But I quickly realized that what the Arab American community needed most was not one Arab American who understood public relations, but a community that needed to understand public relations.

I launched an Arab American newspaper, in English, called *The Middle Eastern Voice*. The intent was to develop a sense of public relations among my community while also exercising public relations and portraying the Arab "cause" to Americans in a positive, clear and concise manner.

But the lesson I tried to teach my community became embedded in my own mind.

The media was against us.

Israel had many writers who were Jewish interpreting their troubles, history and needs in the media.

The Arabs had only a few.

I decided I had to become a journalist.

In adopting journalism as my chosen career, I had also accepted a critical principle of journalism that I would be objective and fair and I would distance myself from partisanship. After being hired as a journalist, and, for more than 15 years, I stood outside of my community watching, trying to provide them a channel of expression whenever I could.

After leaving journalism, I returned to the community and again worked with the Arab organizations that existed.

They included the Arab American Anti-Discrimination Committee, the Arab American Institute and the National Association of Arab Americans.

And, I also worked closely with the handful of Arab American newspapers that published regularly in the United States, sending them articles and urging them to expand their publications by including English articles as well as Arabic language articles.

In 1995, Palestinians from around the country formed the Palestinian American Congress. Chapters were formed in some 14 cities around the country in cities like Los Angeles, San Francisco, New York, New Jersey, Dallas and Chicago. Each chapter elected local officers and also delegates to a national convention that was held in Chicago in May, 1995.

At that convention, as both a local officer in Chicago and a national delegate, I was nominated and unanimously elected as the PAC's first national president.

It was a roller coaster ride that is still difficult to assess.

As a Christian, I was immediately attacked by the defenders of the Hamas Islamicist organization. Their activists labeled me a "Jew" and a "Zionist" because of my outspoken support for the peace process, and because I dared to appear at public meetings with Jewish American leaders. Of course, they also denounced Yasir Arafat and Hanan Ashrawi, too.

One Arab newspaper called me a "Jew" and a "Zionist" and

warned that justice for me would be meted out in other ways than through their printed word.

Some local activists who distributed Hamas literature, launched a continued stream of attacks against me, refusing to support the PAC as long as I was its president.

One writer went so far as to argue that electing a Christian as national president was the same as Americans electing an African American as the president of the United States.

Ironically, on the back page of this mouthpiece for Hamas which constantly lambasted American imperialism, there was a full page ad purchased by MCI, an "American imperialist corporation."

Terrorism is not simply the acting out of violence. It is the direct bi-product of extremism.

The American justice system is so busy stereotyping all Arabs as terrorists that they miss the real activities of extremism and terrorism. The very people who are warning about Hamas infiltration in the United States don't even know what is being published in the Arabic language press, and can't tell the difference between Muslims and Christians, Palestinians and Jordanians, the moderates and the extremists.

My agenda during my term as president was to address these flaws and to educate not only Americans about the truth of our community's problems, but to also educate our community and encourage the silent majority to stand up and speak out.

These selected speeches offer an insight into my focus and the Arab American message.

Outside Looking in

(Speech to Roosevelt University students, Jan. 28, 1995)

Thank you for the invitation to speak to you today. After leaving the Chicago *Sun-Times* I have spent a lot of time working with community and ethnic organizations on how they can increase their involvement and become more effective in this society.

Involvement in this society is very important. And, the two areas of involvement that are the most effective are in the news media, and in government or politics.

I know something about both areas.

I worked as a reporter and journalist for nearly 17 years, first with a community newspaper called The *Daily Southtown Economist* Newspapers, and later with the Chicago *Sun-Times*.

I spent most of those 17 years covering Chicago's City Hall and Chicago area politics.

First, I want to tell you something about two areas of involvement that I believe are essential, and how they are often sidestepped by ethnic communities.

As an Arab American, an ethnic American, I come from a community where families encourage their children to pursue higher education, and aspire to end up in professions such as medicine, dentistry, business and engineering. We have many lawyers, many grocery store owners and many, many doctors.

Those professions are viewed among my ethnic community as honorable. If you become a doctor, it is believed, you have established respect. I'm not talking about the area of *professional* respect, because the greatest respect in the Arab community is respect for family and paternity.

In the Middle East, the professions or careers least respected by the people are those careers involved in the news media and in government.

As an ethnic American, I have learned that all of the various ethnic communities share common experiences, just in different ways. We all have our stories of discrimination, hurdles and even our achievements. Many of us come from countries where Democracy is often not a realistic option or priority.

That's the case in the Middle East, especially among Arab countries.

And, because both journalism and government are offsprings of Democracy, they are frowned upon in the Arab world, and in many foreign countries, especially those considered outside of the Western World, and that are foreign to Democracy.

Government officials and politicians, in most Arab countries, are considered shills for dictators and monarchs. Government is the vehicle by which monarchies and dictatorships control the masses. So, a loving mother would never encourage her son to become a government official ... and since there are few free elections, no one in their right mind would run for public office in an election unless they were already handpicked for service.

Journalists are even worse.

Most journalists in the Middle East, with some exception, are controlled by their local governments. A Free Press is a rarity. They exist, but they are the exception rather than the rule. Dictatorships and monarchies do not permit freedom of expression, which is the essence of journalism and a free press. Without freedom of thought, even in cases where the reporters and columnists are talented, they are not true journalists because they are allowed only to express regardless of talent and cunning, only certain viewpoints. That censorship, or more like a restriction, makes most Arab journalists more or less propagandists for the governments that control them.

So, a loving mother in the Middle East never encourages their children to become reporters either.

I remember when I told my parents I was going to be a reporter, they frowned. When I told them I wanted to cover politics, they fainted. Why couldn't I be something respectful, like a doctor, or even a grocery store owner?

Which brings me to my point ... the greatest points of influence in this country begin with government and journalism.

The media in this country defines everything that we touch, breath or dream.

What we say is mulched by the media, spit out and refashioned in their own eyes.

If among those eyes ... are none of your people ... then the product is biased, skewered, incomplete, and discriminatory.

That is the case for most ethnic communities, especially Arab Americans.

In this country, most people learn everything they know about foreign countries, foreigners and ethnics from what they read in the local newspapers or what they hear on the radio or see on television.

(In the context of the media, I also include Hollywood, which defines in a more precise fashion our images and how we look to others.)

So, if I were to ask you, how many of you wish to help your own people become more involved in this country?

I would answer that the most effective way is to become journalists and government officials. Run for public office. Seek reporting and journalism jobs.

Politicians feed into the media and they define how society treats you. If you are involved, as a community, in both levels, then and only then can you be guaranteed that government services, which are paid for by your taxes, will be fairly distributed to service the needs of your community.

This influence also impacts not only on local issues, such as social programs, but also on international policy.

I deal with this problem in the Arab community all the time.

First, many Arabs that I know believe that getting involved in local politics is a waste of time because it does not impact on international politics ... as if there is anything that we, as individuals, can do to impact international politics.

However, a politically conscious community can influence international policy, national policy and local policy.

I ran for public office in 1992. I knew that I couldn't win, but I also knew that only 1 out of every 100 Arab Americans in this country are registered to vote. That is compared to the average of 2 in three Americans who are registered to vote, which is the norm. That doesn't mean that everyone registered to vote who is qualified to register to vote, actually goes to the polls. They don't. But that is besides the point, or at least the subject of another topic discussion.

Many people think that running for public office is a horrible experience. It is. Politics is like living in a fish bowl. Your whole life becomes exposed to the world. In communities like the Arab community, privacy and family are sacred. Having your life exposed as mine was is sacrilegious. And my life was exposed. Supporters of my opponent distributed literature that claimed that I was an Iraqi. This was just after Desert Storm and and the war with Iraq. Nice guy. I lost. But for a first try running as a Democrat in a predominantly Republican district, I did very well.

I learned as a very young person that the media is where the power is. And power is how communities can get involved and protect themselves and secure the proper services.

At an early age, I debated Israeli Foreign Minister Abba Eban on national television. I was very effective. My presentation was effective. Abba Eban is considered one of the most eloquent spokesmen in the world.

In this country, perception is reality. Ninety percent of what a person believes is, in their mind, true. And, their perception comes from the media. It also comes from familiarity. People who represent you, who look and sound like you, "the average

American," are the most effective people to represent you.

Americans want to feel comfortable. Most Americans could care less about your international problems or even your community problems. Why should an American want to know anything more about Palestine than Chechnya or Biafra or Pakistan? They listen to people who look and sound like themselves, and they distance themselves most from people who seem strange or different. If you act and sound different, the greater the odds that your message will not be heard. The more you look and sound like the American you are trying to influence, the more effective you will be in getting their attention, their sympathy and their support.

I did a live radio talk show on WLS for many years. One time, I was invited to participate in a debate between an Israeli spokesman and an Iraqi spokesman. The Israeli spokesman began by offering a very coherent, rational and calm explanation of his country's position. He acted and sounded just like the typical person listening to the radio show. He sounded American.

The Iraqi, however, was a different story. His problem was typical of what many minorities and ethnics bring upon themselves through their inability to overcome their frustration.

He started his statement by declaring, "Look, I get very emotional and angry and I don't care what that guys says." He had a heavy accent. His English was broken. He did in fact get emotional. No American is going to listen to a guy like that.

That's why a "terrorist" like Menachem Begin can get away with his deeds and a "terrorist" like Yasir Arafat is so hated by the rest of the world. I'm not calling either a terrorist, by the way, but I am referring to how they are viewed by their critics.

Begin looked and acted like an American in many ways. Arafat needs a shave. And you know something, most Americans can't seem to get past that five-day stubble to understand what in the hell Arafat is talking about.

Now, you may say that the failure of the American public to look past superficial issues, to look beyond their perception, to see the real substance of an issue is in fact their flaw.

It may very well be true. But it is also reality. And reality decides American public opinion. Reality decides government policy, such as how much money is given to different communities or to different countries. Reality decides whether your community gets what it deserves or is ignored by your local government officials.

I once studied under a great man, a political scientist who spent a lot of time teaching me about Chicago politics, Milton Rakove.

Professor Rakove once wrote a book on Chicago politics, *Don't Make No Waves, Don't Back No Losers.* In it, he said that most Chicago politicians ignore the needs and views and concerns of the Arab community. He concluded, it didn't matter, because most Arabs don't vote.

In the legislative district where I ran for office in 1992, there is an estimated Arab population of about 4,000 families. Fewer than 40, an insignificant number, were registered to vote.

This isn't about convincing you that you should register to vote.

It is beyond that. What I am talking about is involvement, and getting involved in the most effective manner. True, being a doctor is important. Being a lawyer is important, too.

But being at the controls of the professions that determine perception and reality are in fact the most important areas of involvement that you, as students, can focus.

You want the Chicago *Sun-Times* to report the news that you think is important, then you had better be a part of that system. Understand the system. Learn how to use it.

If not, then you will be a victim of that system.

Always remember, that you must live the perception in order to successfully sell the reality to the American public.

A Vote for Moderation

(Acceptance Speech as President of the Palestinian American Congress, PAC, Ramada Congress Hotel, May 27, 1995.)

I want to first thank all of you for your vote of confidence. A vote of confidence not only in me and in my dedication to the Palestinian cause, but also for your vote of confidence in our future.

My election tonight symbolizes a major refocus of Palestinian activism in this country. Tonight, with my election, you are passing on a torch of responsibility for our people in this country to a Palestinian American who not only is born in this country but who is educated, assimilated and influenced by the American system of Democracy, fairness and free Speech.

That is not to say that as a Palestinian American born in Chicago, that I have forgotten that my father, *Allah Yarhamu*, his family and his parents were born in Jerusalem, Palestine; that they owned a home in the Romema Quarter of Jerusalem and that they owned land outside of Jerusalem that today is an exclusive Jewish settlement.

That is not to say, that as a Palestinian American born in Chicago, that I have forgotten that my mother, *Allah Yarhamha*, her family and her parents were born in Bethlehem and lived in a home that today is still under an occupation that has changed hands from the Ottoman Empire to the British Mandate to Israeli Occupation.

That is not to say that while I have embraced as fully as one can the spirit of this country, that I am not rooted in a deep love and loyalty to the culture, heritage and needs of my people .... Palestinians wrongly uprooted from their national homeland, Palestine, and who have dispersed and settled in countries around the world, including in this country.

That is not to say that as a Palestinian born in this country, that I do not fully understand the priorities of the Palestinian People in this country.

Because I am American born, I understand them even more than many of you who were born in Palestine, who lived in Palestine ... who speak Arabic and who live and think the Palestinian identity.

As an American born Palestinian, I have had to struggle twice as hard to prove my dedication to my people, handicapped by never having lived in Palestine and by the fact that English is my primary language.

But these handicaps on my ethnicity and national identity are in fact the power that I will use to give Palestinians in this country a new strong voice. A voice that understands the American system of Politics. A voice that understands the American system of Democracy. And a voice that recognizes the importance that Americans in this country place upon image, perception and the delivery of a message.

I will deliver our message of Palestinian Inalienable rights in this country in a way that it has never been delivered before, standing with a unified Palestinian American Congress that is founded on principles of Unity, Democracy and equality.

And, what is our message as Palestinian Americans?

Our message is that the Palestinian People deserve nothing less than the right of return to our homeland, Palestine, with Jerusalem as its capitol.

Our message is that the injustices of 47 years of national expulsion must end.

Our message to the world is that we, as American Palestinians, have a role to play in this country and we will use that role and responsibility to restore our national rights to a homeland ... and that we will never forget the lessons of the Oklahoma City bombing, that no matter how long that we live in this country. No matter how hard that we work in this country. No matter whether we served in the US Military to defend this country. People in this country will still see us as foreigners. They will discriminate against us, and blame us and incite against us, unless we stand up for ourselves and demand that it stop.

My right as a Palestinian American is as great as any American in this country. I will accept no less than my full rights to express myself and to advocate forcefully on behalf of the rights of the Palestinian People. And I will do this in every city in this country. I will take this message to the Congress where Anti-Arab legislation that panders to the special interest vote must end and where ignorantly proposed and unjustly drafted legislation to move the US Embassy from Tel Aviv to Jerusalem must be stopped dead in its tracks.

My agenda as the National President of the Palestine American Congress is our agenda, and I accept it from you as the mandate that will guide our efforts in every step.

First, I will work to strengthen and organize Palestine American Congress chapters throughout the United States.

I will work hard and with a vigor that is unmatched to win over the support of those Palestinians, Muslim and Christian in this country who have yet to recognize the historic significance of this new movement that we have started today.

I will reach out to every sector of the Palestinian community, blind to individual politics, and uninfluenced even by my own personal political views, to convince those Palestinians who now stand on the outside of our community to join with us as one voice, one people, for one goal.

I will push to establish direct communications between the National Board of Congress persons, and to carry our agenda directly to the White House and to the US Congress.

My priority this first year will be to help solidify a foundation for a process of Democracy that is blind to individual political views and allegiances, and is dedicated to only one priority, the rights of the Palestinians to return to their National Homeland, and the necessity to better organize the Palestinians in this Country to work toward that singular, long term goal.

I believe that we must work with our young Palestinians who are also born in this country and who are becoming lost by our inability to galvanize our community, to lead them back to Palestinian National identity and help them merge this Palestinian loyalty into the American system. Not only as doctors, lawyers, grocers and engineers, but also as Journalists who influence the media, public relations specialists who influence public opinion and perception, and candidates who will continue to win election to public office where they can end the inherent discrimination that exists against Palestinian Americans, Arab Americans, both Christian and Muslim.

In the past, we were many voices, divided by our political differences. In the past, we were individual political organizations working toward the same goal in different ways.

In the past, we each grabbed the chain of our oppression at different points, each determined but always unsuccessful.

Today, however, through this process of Democracy and unity, we look toward the future as:

One voice.

One vision.

One dedication.

We Haven't Done Enough

*(Speech to the San Francisco Chapter
of the PAC, Sept. 29, 1995.)*

Ladies and Gentlemen, our community is in crisis. We face a crisis internally, and one from outside. If we don't work together, we may perish as a community ... perish by our own hand, because of our failure to do what is needed as a community in this country.

Our culture and our heritage is under siege. In the West Bank. In the Arab World. In the United States. Just look around.

In Libya, 350 Palestinians are arrested and deported. Thousands of other Palestinians are being threatened.

Similar expulsions, crackdowns and persecution is occurring in Jordan, Egypt, Syria, Lebanon and in our own Arab countries.

The same kind of persecution that occurs in the West Bank, in our own homeland.

And, it is here, too, in the United States.

Just look around us.

Musa Abu-Marzook is only the latest Palestinian singled out for discrimination and political persecution.

Others in this country scoff at us, because they have greater influence over the news media. So no one hears our story.

The Wall Street Journal, The New York Times, The Washington Post, The Chicago Tribune ... they all refuse to tell our side of the story.

But it is also our fault.

Abu Marzook is in jail today because we have not done our job.

We have to accept some of the responsibility for this Palestinian tragedy.

We can't close our eyes to them and pretend they are not occurring. We can't sit back, afraid to tell the truth.

But the truth is also painful for ourselves.

We have not done enough to protect ourselves.

If our community were strong.

If we spoke with one voice on issues of general acceptance and consensus.

If we worked with each other instead of against each other.

If we learned to respect our differences instead of using them to divide our community further ...

The Federal Government is psychic when it comes to our crimes.

They don't need evidence to charge us.

They don't need proof to lock us up.

They don't even need to follow the meticulous judicial process that is prostrated for everyone else ... just look at how meticulous the process is in protecting the crimes of OJ Simpson ... more than one year, bending over backwards, microscopic media scrutiny ... but when the accused is a Palestinian, like Musa Abu Marzook, the law is inconsequential. The law and the process doesn't exist for us.

So they can roust him in the middle of the night. Steal him away from his family ... shackle him, bound him, and thrust him in a dark prison cell, far enough away from judicial due process to break his morale, and weaken his ability to defend himself.

And where are we, the Palestinian American Community?

We all stand up, individually, and cry foul.

We all, individually, denounce what has occurred.

No organization. No muscle. Small collections of whispers in the dark, demanding justice from people who cannot hear us.

Our division is so great, we might as well be silent.

But our silence is not only a disservice to ourselves, it is a disservice to prisoners of conscience like Musa Abu Marzook, who sits in a cell, a political pawn in a political game of chess. Another statistic that continues to build ... another Palestinian in jail.

We are so busy attacking each other that we can't hear the cries of the people who are suffering.

The Palestinian American Congress is an attempt to respond to these problems.

The symptoms are clear. Division. Emotion. Disunity. Internal conflict.

The disease is obvious. Ineffectiveness. National dysfunction. Community chaos.

We need to set aside our differences, join hand in hand, and agree to focus on the greater issues that bring us together and ignore those small issues that keep us apart.

We need to bring together the small islands of Palestinian existence -- the Ramallah Federation, the Al Bireh Society, the Bethlehem Society, the Fatah, the Jabha, the Islamicists, the Muslims, Christians and the independents ... because as individual groups, we are small voices, heard loudly by each other, but mute to the rest of the world.

The Palestinian American Congress is different from all of these organizations for a very special reason.

It declares itself involved in the politics of the United States.

It declares itself founded on the principle of Democracy.

It declares that every Palestinian, regardless of background, has an equal voice in this process of fairness.

Because we are dedicated to supporting the process, not the individual.

When I am gone, someone else from our community will continue to lead us.

The individual is insignificant to the movement.

The process is the strength.

In the United States, Democracy augments the voices of the weak.

Small, self-interest groups like our own, suddenly become major players in this country through Democracy.

We elect leaders. We base our goals on elections and an electoral process, and the American media listens.

But they are so used to brushing us off, that even when we face a major issue that is unparalleled in this country's judicial system, such as the illegal arrest of Musa Abu Marzook, they turn their backs on us ... unless we force them to listen.

In this country, perception is reality.

Reality is not reality to Americans who live by what they hear on the radio, read in the newspapers, and watch on television.

Hollywood is the great American University of knowledge, where just causes are slain and the wrong are elevated to positions of prominence.

We know our cause is just.

But we also know that this country is the key, the future of the Middle East, and since 1948 has directed the movement of facts in Palestine.

We must now merge these two truths into one, using a movement of strength. Bringing our people together.

Focussing on strategies of common sense.

Does anyone control the American News Media when it comes to the Middle East?

Yes, but only in the sense of influence.

But, it is our uninvolvement that controls the media. We allow the news media to write what it writes because we don't take the right steps to respond.

We allow the US Government to violate our rights, because we have not used the instruments of Democracy to strengthen our voices and build our community.

My views as an individual are insignificant. But our views as a community can move mountains.

What is important is the process that I am involved in to strengthen Democracy in our community.

You can join this movement tonight.

We have organized chapters in more than 22 American cities.

Although we are only four months old, we continue to grow.

We don't have a lot of money and our administration is still learning to walk.

Four hundred people here tonight demonstrates that we want a change from the past. More than 400 of you here tonight are saying that we have to do something different.

The San Francisco Chapter, here tonight, is one of the strongest chapters in the United States. But we also have chapters in Chicago, Dallas, Los Angeles, Detroit, Cleveland, Washington, New York, Philadelphia ...

One of our first programs this year is to focus our community on the issue of Jerusalem.

Jerusalem is the heart of the Middle East conflict and the Question of Palestine.

It doesn't matter whether is a peace process or not.

What matters is that the face of Palestine continues to change, and we must ask ourselves are we ready to recognize that change is taking place? And, are we ready to recognize that we must deal with the reality of these changes?

Everyday since 1948, we have seen the face of Palestine change.

We have to become involved and help stop these changes, to preserve our country and our national identity.

As Palestinian Americans, we must do a better job of informing the American people, who control the politicians and who influence the media.

They are the key.

In this country, the politician listens to the people on issues of foreign policy.

Nov. 12 through Nov. 18 is Jerusalem Week.

Palestinians around the country will organize events in their cities to recognize the significance of Jerusalem as a Palestinian City, and will organize information campaigns to begin the process of re-educating Americans on the truth of Jerusalem and Palestine.

A national symposium will be held by the Congress in Washington on Nov. 17th, to reinforce this process, including speakers from around the world, Muslim and Christian, re-educating the world on the historical facts, not fantasies of Jerusalem's existence.

It's our responsibility to become involved and to make sure that the message goes out loud and clear to all.

We have a right to Jerusalem.

And, Jerusalem must be the capitol of our Palestine State.

Israel has no right to continue to discriminate against Christians and Muslims, prohibiting them from entering Jerusalem. Israel has no right to continue to evict Palestinians from Jerusalem, and implementing policies that are designed to discourage our community's natural growth in Jerusalem, and to forcibly erase our history, in much the same manner that the early Nazis attempted to erase the historical existence of Jews in 1930s Europe.

We can work together and we can be successful.

Arab Political Empowerment

(Speech to the Muslim Public Affairs Council,
Northwestern University,May 14, 1994.)

M y job is to help people better prepare themselves to be candidates for public office in the Chicago area, so I am going tonight to pretend that you have hired me to be your political consultant, not just for a campaign, but for overall image enhancement.

And, why did you hire me?

Because there are 400,000 Muslims in the Chicagoland area of various ethnic backgrounds, and there is not one Muslim that holds public office in that same area that we know of. In fact, there are only two people who have sought or who are seeking election in this election cycle that are Muslim.

I will tell you what I tell all of my clients, and it doesn't specifically address your environment as Muslims, but it does address your predicament as a group that has been "left out" or "shut out" of the political process.

There two points you must understand in order to enhance your involvement in the political process and in the larger society.

A.   Perception is 90 percent of reality.

What people believe is most often what is important to them. How they view you as people is more important in many cases than how they view your basic message, in your case, your Islamic activism and Muslim-based idealogies.

B.   The Message IS NOT as important in the United States as is the means that you use to deliver the message ... and this is only true if your priority here as Muslims in America is to influence American public opinion. If that is not your priority, and your priority audience is maintaining Muslim allegiance or the Muslim community as a whole, then the message IS the priority.

But, if your priority is to influence Americans, the message must be superseded by the means of delivery.

Both perception and the means of delivery work together.

Americans are generally a very shallow society. Very materialistic. Their concerns are the self, in most cases. They stereotype and base their images on what they see more often than on what they hear. Their stereotypes are formed by Hollywood and the News Media, and, in general, Arabs and Muslims are not viewed as distinguishable people. They are seen as one.

In general, Americans are concerned about buying a new car, about caring for their family, about protecting what is theirs, and also with strengthening their own self image as the protectors of the world, even though in practice their actions subjugate more people than free them.

Ask an American what is important to them, and you will not get a good answer. Ask a Muslim or an Arab, and the answer is more clearly defined.

And when you understand this difference, you must then understand that how you present yourself to Americans is more important than what you are telling them.

That is a mistake that Arabs and Muslims have made for generations in their efforts to influence American public opinion.

Our spokespeople must represent the message and the perception of what Americans want to hear

And what do Americans want? They want someone who looks like them, talks like them, sounds like them and understands them to tell them what is right.

They are immediately turned on or turned off by the appearance of the messenger.

If you sound foreign, or if their first impression of you is Islam or Arabism, they will tune you out ... we're stereotyping, but we are talking about the majority of Americans.

In order to influence Americans, you must be able to get them to listen to your message. Once you get them to hear your message, they will support you in most cases. It is always the same.

When a Palestinian, for example, and an American get to know each other as neighbors, or as co-workers, they become friends. Once they become friends, the American is almost always receptive and sympathetic to the suffering of the Palestinians and they often will express that sympathy in militant activism in support of Palestinian rights.

But when that same person turns on a TV set and sees a Palestinian arguing the issues, they are immediately turned off especially when they see the Palestinian spokesman resemble the stereotype of a foreigner.

It isn't enough to speak out on issues ... you must be able to do more in American society.

Oftentimes, the Muslim community is drawn into heated issues debates that are defined by others. We need to define our own issues, and the most effective way to do that is to become a part of the system.

And, to become a part of the system, you must again address the problem of how the message is delivered.

Muslims and Arabs must improve their means of communication. Communication is the key to influence in this country, and it is often the means of delivering the message ... at least they work together.

We Arabs and Muslims have very few newspapers that can be called "journalistic", and instead we have too many newspapers filled with propaganda and rhetoric that is intended for the wrong audiences. Our Arab and Muslim newspapers and media often times spend all their energies on addressing "The Choir." In other words, we spend all our time telling our own people what is right, instead or focussing on the people who disagree with us or do not understand us.

Our media must begin to reflect this issue, and address the non-Muslim and Non-Arab society.

We as Muslims and Arabs are not represented in the news media. Part of the reason for this shortfall is our own fault. We all want our children to be doctors, lawyers and engineers. No one wants their son or daughter to be a reporter, or a Hollywood movie producer. Yet while doctors, lawyers and engineers generate decent wages, the reporter and the Hollywood producer are the most effective professions in terms of influencing American society.

Is there bias in the news media?

Yes, but partly because we allow the bias to exist by not learning how to participate in the proper way.

Is the media "controlled by Jews?"

No. The media is influenced by the people who are involved in the media profession, and the media will denigrate those people who have the least involvement.

These are some of the points that must be understood before we enter the political arena where the real decisions about our lives are made.

Lastly, I want to say that many of you are probably sitting out there saying that you want to be Muslim first and Americans second. I say that it is your responsibility to make the sacrifice in order that others that follow may have a better life in this country and that the concerns of Muslims and Arabs flourish and are better understood.

You have to sacrifice ... not by compromising in your ideals, but by accepting that the above techniques are critical to your success in achieving the primary objective of influencing Americans.

If you make the sacrifice today, by being Americans first, your children will not have to sacrifice tomorrow.

A Vision of Peace

(Speech to Hadassah, Chicago, April 11, 1994)

L adies and gentlemen:
Thank you so much for your invitation today, and also for giving me the opportunity to address you.

One of my main priorities since leaving the Chicago *Sun-Times* and ending an 18 year career as a journalist, is to help strengthen the voices of moderates in the Palestinian and Arab American communities.

I can tell you from personal experience that it is not easy being a moderate Palestinian. We are criticized by the extremists who have held our community hostage to their acts of terrorism for too many years.

But, if that were my only problem with being a moderate. As a moderate, we are ignored by the American press.

The Jewish Community, for many years, painted Palestinians with one broad brush. If we didn't recognize Israel's right to exist, then we were terrorists too!

Hollywood is the worst ... casting every terrorist film part with someone who looks like one of my uncles. And, while there are more than 150 movies that portray Arabs and Palestinians as bloodthirsty murderers and cowardly killers, there is only one movie that paints a positive picture of an Arab, and it is called *Aladdin*.

Why am I a moderate? Maybe it's because I grew up in a Jewish community as a young child on Chicago's Southeast Side in South Shore Valley.

I attended the Henry Horn Jewish Community Center dances, although I was denied membership, when it was located at 91st and Jeffery. I sat at Mel Markon's restaurant at 92nd and Jeffery with my friends, Jeff, Sheldon, Michael, Jack, and Jay. We talked about things that kids talked about.

But I think that I am a moderate because I believe that there is a way for Arab and Jew to live together in the same land, as neighbors and as friends.

Before I offer a Palestinian's perspective of the historical overview of the period leading up to the Israel/PLO Peace Accord, I want to give you my vision of what may come 15 years down the road if peaceful negotiations continue.

I see an Israel and a Palestine as two separate states, side by side.

Israel would exist formally in the territories, generally, prior to the 1967 war.

Palestine would exist formally in the majority of what we call the West Bank and Gaza Strip.

Jerusalem would be the capitol of both Nations, shared and revered equally, administered by both.

Jews in Israel would have full rights of citizenship in the State of Israel. The affairs of Israel would be decided by its Jewish citizens.

Christian and Moslem Palestinians would have full rights to citizenship in the Palestinian State. The affairs of Palestine would be decided by it's Christian and Moslem citizens.

Jewish citizens of Israel could live in the West Bank or the Gaza Strip with the status of "residents." They could lease land. They could operate businesses, but they could not vote in Palestinian elections, nor could they hold public office in Palestine.

In Israel, Palestinian Christians and Moslems could also live as "residents" under the same basic guidelines.

Jerusalem would have a municipal council consisting equally of Jews on one side and Palestinian Christians and Moslems on the other. There would be one mayor, Jew or Palestinian, elected by residents of each country by weighted vote.

Both Israel and Palestine would claim Jerusalem, rightly, as their capitol. For Jerusalem, there can be no other way.

Sounds idealistic, doesn't it? Maybe. But, we have already seen the alternative. One-hundred years of bloodshed. Forty-five years of a defacto state of war for the country that was supposed to be created as a haven of safety for Jews from around the world.

We have no other choice but to sit down with each other and negotiate a peace accord. We shouldn't bargain like tourist and shopkeepers in a bazaar. We should negotiate as equals. We should work not only toward a compromise, but a compromise that satisfies the most people on both sides.

Why did Israel and the PLO finally sit down to discuss peace?

Several factors made it possible. The ultra-conservative Likud Party was replaced by the Labor Party governing Israel. That was an important change.

The Iraq War and Desert Storm were major factors, too. Although the world disarmed Saddam Hussein, and put him in check, the war itself created a major upheaval among the radical element and thought in some quarters of the Arab World, and particularly among the more extreme elements of the Muslim community.

The PLO was on the verge of disintegration as a result of its stand in support of the Iraqi people.

You see, even as a moderate Palestinian who, by the way, served in the United States Air Force during the end of the Vietnam War, I have a view of what happened that is easily distorted into one of extremism. Saddam Hussein's invasion of Kuwait and the subsequent murders of Kuwaiti citizens was criminal. But, the bombing of Iraq went far beyond what was necessary, and the harshness of the embargo today is punishing not Saddam Hussein but the Iraqi people.

Iraq was always a friend to the Palestinians, and I might point out was also a friend to the United States when we needed Iraq to keep Iran in check.

Yasir Arafat's limited support of Saddam Hussein during the war may have been inappropriate and unwise, but it was necessary on his part.

Hamas was slowly rising not only among the Palestinian community as a major force, but Islamic extremism was building strength too.

As a side note on this point ... I was really angry when I learned that Baruch Goldstein, a doctor sworn to save lives, was able to change his bullet clip four times before he was finally subdued by survivors at the Hebron Mosque. I was angry when told that Hebron's Palestinians pleaded with Rabin to subdue Goldstein in a letter nearly one year before. The tragedy could have been averted.

But, I also strongly condemn the killings of Israelis in Afula by Hamas ... and a young 19 year old Ra'id Zakarina, I mourn for him because the real killers were the Hamas leaders who were allowed to manipulate this young man into believing that taking innocent lives is a proper revenge for Goldstein's acts. I am shamed by the Hamas statement that the Afula murders were "an heroic suicide mission."

We have to change the way we view terrorism ... we can't give it an ethnic or religious identity. And, we have to stop calling the victims of terrorists Jews or Arabs. They are people.

Another factor that moved Israel and the PLO together was the Intifadah. The Palestinian Uprising has cost Israel dearly. And, it posed a greater long-term threat to Israel. The focal point of the Palestinian elite was shifting from the PLO, which was based in Tunis, to the young Palestinians in the West Bank and the Gaza Strip. It is a protracted uprising, and results do not come quick when your main weapon is David's stone. But in the long run, it was producing a much more determined and more radical Palestinian element.

It's in this context that Israel, in my opinion, made a major policy shift, agreeing to negotiate formally with the Palestine Liberation Organization. You see, the PLO has always wanted to negotiate with Israel. But the PLO and Israel have two different fan clubs. On the Israeli side, the Government of Israel could shift gears and deal with criticism because it has a broader base of support. The PLO, on the other hand, must deal with a growing body of extremism, and extremists who do not hesitate to deal in death.

Those extremists are not giving up easily on either side.

The Israeli PLO Peace Accord calls for many things to begin: It allows the Palestinians to begin the restoration of their self-respect and dignity by allowing them to serve as their own police force ... and by allowing them to assume autonomy for health, education, welfare, taxation and tourism, first in Jericho and the Gaza Strip.

Issues of utilities, finance, transportation and industrial development, and the creation of new jobs in the West Bank and Gaza Strip will be handled by an Israeli-Palestinian Economic Cooperation Committee. The issue of Jerusalem will be addressed three years from the beginning of autonomy. During a five year period of Palestinian self-rule, Israeli soldiers which symbolize the occupation, will be redeployed outside populated areas of the West Bank. By the end of the first year, Palestinians will elect their own Council to run the West Bank and Gaza Strip, with Palestinians from East Jerusalem participating as voters.

The Peace Accord may sound like little more than a vision -- but for all of us, it should be hope.

Israel has made it easy for the extremists on the Palestinian side. Israel has ruled with a double standard toward Palestinians.

How do you think it makes me feel when I am told as a Palestinian American visitor to my parent's homeland, that my ID card has to have a special marking ... that my car has to have a special license plate ... that the policy of the Israeli Defense Forces is to not intervene if they witness a Jewish Settler shooting Palestinians, until the settler runs out of ammunition ... that Jewish Settlers are allowed to carry automatic weapons and prowl the streets of Arab areas as if in a formal provocation, begging for violence.

You can point to many extreme acts of terrorism by Palestinians ... but frustration is a heavy burden on any people ... and when the frustration is too great, acts of rebellion turn into acts of terror. The

Jewish community understands frustration ... we saw it at the Warsaw Ghetto and at Masada. It is better to die with dignity than to live with shame.

I don't intend to demean the special circumstances of the Holocaust or to suggest that the death camps of Nazi Germany were anything remotely similar to Israel's treatment of Palestinians.

But how can a people who survived the Holocaust close their eyes to injustices and maltreatment of Palestinian civilians?

End the frustration, eliminate the shame. The mighty should be magnanimous.

Perception is Reality

(Speech to the ADC, September 4, 1993,
Chicago Hilton & Towers Hotel)

There used to be an old saying in the American Arab community ... an excuse, rather, that was repeated as often as Israel won its military battles against the Arab World. It went something like this: The Israelis have a bad case but great lawyers, while the Arabs have a great case, but lousy lawyers.

You see, the Arab who defined that witty little saying obviously doesn't understand where the problem is. No wonder we've been losing the war, if they concentrate all their resources on lawyers.

Instead, the saying should be: The Israelis have a lousy case, and a great public relations firm, and a lot of friends in the news media. And, no matter what they do, they still look like winners in the headlines.

Headlines and news stories have a lot to do with how the *video software, computer literate I need my information short fast and to the point, rock and roll rap music, CD-ROM, 32-bit chip, 640 K Memory, typical American* wants it! Short and sweet. Neatly wrapped. To the point.

They don't want to be bothered with the boring details of true tragedy ... they have seen and read it all ... they want to be surprised ... they want to be captivated with something new ... they want to read and watch TV reports about people they know, usually Hollywood celebrities.

The tragedy of the Palestinian people doesn't fit the typical American bill ... it isn't tragedy enough. And on top of it all, the people Americans want to feel sorry for must look like them.

Isn't that why the world takes it's time to feel sorry for the

Bosnians? Because the world can't decide whether they are Third World, because of their Muslim religions, or Anglo based on their blue eyed blond haired looks.

We sit and watch babies being massacred and women and children murdered in Bosnia every day on TV. Tragedy isn't enough to motivate a people to come to someone's defense. There has to be an enemy, someone to hate. When you give the American people someone to hate, they will rally behind the victims. Throw in a little guilt on top of it, and they will also send lots of money.

Isn't that why the Americans and the Western world sided with Israel?

And let's face it ... the American audience is the audience we should be addressing ... particularly in the post-Communist era ... with the disintegration of the Soviet Communist system and the Western World's greatest devil. The Soviet devil is no longer there. And that is the bad news for the Arabs because we are among the last remaining villains in Western eyes.

Now, it is even tougher on us, and more reason why we must concentrate our resources here in the United States, the world's single, most influential superpower.

The Western World hates the Arabs. They hate the Muslims, who are the symbol of the Arab World. And they don't care whether or not many of those Arabs are Christian. To most Americans they might as well be Muslims. They can't tell us apart. Muslim or Christian. Palestinian or Jordanian. Syrian or Iraqi.

And you can't truly understand why we can't get media support until we recognize some of these facts. Inherently, the media is a business that wants to sell news. The basic principle is that people buy news that they want to read. They don't buy news they don't want to read. Americans like to read about catastrophe. They don't like to read about good news. And that is why the newspapers are filled with bad news stories, and only fleeting, patronizing stories about good news.

To understand this media trap, you also have to understand the true parameters of the media monster. It just doesn't include the newspapers, radio or television stations. The media problem is a multi-media problem.

The media, like everyone else in this country, learns about major issues through the one common denominator in American intellectual understanding and education: dramatic television and television entertainment, and through the movie theaters, which are the parents of television.

And who controls the movies?

Hollywood. That's where the distortion starts and it weaves its way through a maze of multi-media avenues, including computer and video software games. In every instance, one of the greatest and most threatening of villains is the Arab, wrapped in sinister, flowing robes and clutching evil intentions in their teeth.

I remember reading magazine articles written by Freda Kirchway in *The Nation* Magazine from 1947 and 1948, where she described the villainous Arabs whose "little brown fingers" poised nervously on the triggers of their rifles as they aimed their guns at the poor, little defenseless Israeli settler pioneers who made the desert bloom with westernization and real civilization.

And then in 1967, *Time* Magazine published Arab jokes to celebrate in the international humiliation of the Arabs.

Everyone has seen the movie *Exodus*, one of the greatest multi-media distortions of historical fact ever produced on celluloid. But to Americans, it is the Bible in their eyes.

Today, the greatest enemy of the Palestinian people is not the ghost of Menachem Begin or his Irgun followers who have been renamed the Likud. It is Chuck Norris, who has contributed to the demonization of the Arab image. And, it's HBO, one of the most racist film makers in the world. Hollywood has caused the death of more Arabs than Israel's army of occupation. We flexed our muscle recently and forced Walt Disney to alter some racist lyrics in the middle of a cartoon song that most children who saw the movie never really understood anyway. But, we allow Chuck Norris to continue to make racist films, and HBO to continue to portray negative, anti-Arab stereotypes in their made-for-cable movies. Paramount and Universal are also involved in this wholesale slaughter of the Arab image in this country, and we can't do a thing about it.

Let's not forget the New York publishing houses that churn out a steady stream of anti-Arabism. The battle for image is being waged right under our noses, on the morning and evening rush hour commuter trains among the passengers who clutch their little styrofoam cups of coffee and are reading their fiction, anti-Arab novels. And it's being waged in the privacy of some suburban bedroom, where a housewife is digesting a romance novel filled with anti-Arab stereotypes.

It's a multi-media assault that began decades ago and that continues against the image of the Arabs. And what do we do? We play into it.

We play in to it when we shut ourselves out from the media, and cite specious arguments that the media is controlled ... controlled by who?

We mistakenly confuse the word "control" with the real word, "influence." In the West, people *influence* the media. They don't control it. Some influence it more than others.

No one controls the media. It's just the other way around. The victims are the people who don't participate in the multi-media circus.

The Palestinian issue is much like a product in this multi-media world of ours. It sounds so insensitive. But for once, can't we in the Arab American community discuss an issue without getting emotional? Without losing our cool?

In a business, when you develop a product, you don't put it in a briefcase and hope that someone discovers it. Fads are discovered, like the hoola hoop. Our case is not a fad.

You have to market it. You have to tell people about it. You have to determine a marketing strategy by evaluating all the potential options.

Let me just tell the skeptics here this morning:

The proof is in the pudding. So far armed struggle, violence, and the absence of a public relations strategy has not worked. In fact, it has made our situation worse. The old ways don't work anymore. They have failed. It's been 45 years since the State of Israel was created, and the only progress has been the slow annexation of Palestinian land, the deportation of hundreds of thousands of Palestinians ... and the brutalization of our Palestinian culture and society. The old ways are not working.

Everyday, the skyline of Jerusalem becomes more Jewish and less Palestinian. We cry about it, but we do nothing about it.

And what are our options?

Let's stop pretending we are in the Middle East. I was there several times and I saw the horrible conditions that our people must endure; while we sit here in the comfort of our hundred thousand dollar homes, we want to tell the people in the West Bank what is in their best interests? Come on.

Our job is right here in the United States. And the sooner we recognize that the better. We have to initiate contact with the media on a very personal level. We have to aggressively lobby the media. And learn the system. And become involved in the media. We have to become players in the media profession. We have to pressure the media to hire Arab Americans as reporters, radio announcers and talk show hosts, and television anchors and reporters.

If the media is where most Americans get their understanding of the world, doesn't it make sense to make an investment in the media?

Here, again, are some basic rules that we must adopt.

1.   Stop making excuses about the media--excuses we use to hide behind or to cover up our own incompetency. No one controls the media. The claim itself is racist and anti-Semitic, and it further damages our image.

2.   Start recognizing that the media is like any other

profession. We have doctors and lawyers and engineers by the hundreds. Yet, we only have a handful of Arab Americans that are reporters. We need to continue to motivate our children to seek journalism careers.

3.   Recognize the basic principle of public relations. First. You sacrifice the self for the cause. In other words, you put the cause above yourself. And, you assimilate into the audience you are trying to influence. You want to convince an American that the Palestinian cause is just ... look, sound and act like an American and stop acting like a stranger when you address them. You have to wrap your message in a cloak of familiarity. Familiarity is what gets you through the door in this country, into the hearts and minds of the typical American.

I always refer back to the image of Yasir Arafat trying to explain our cause to the American people. While he is explaining the history of our struggle, the American audience is fixated on his stubbled chin, his heavy, Middle East accent, and his explosive, rhetoric filled diatribe. And, they remember the empty holster at the United Nations in 1976.

But few Americans remember his message.

Bad public relations.

But that bad public relations has been repeated over and over again.

4.   Learn the system. Learn who the editors are and who the reporters are. Understand the process required to write a press release, focus on the message, and convey that message to the news media. It's simple.

5.   Incorporate a budget for public relations into your organizations. You have to spend money to get media attention. A typical Public Relations budget should be 15 percent of your annual operating budget.

6.   Separate the spokesman from the activist. The spokesman is the person who is most like the audience you are trying to influence.

7.   Finally, we have to develop our own community news

media. We need a news media that addresses the American audience with rational, reasoned material, not a media that relies on emotional, gossipy trash written in Arabic.

Aren't we talking to the wrong people in our Arab American press?

We need a real ethnic press that is professional and journalistic in approach and style and quality. We have some good newspapers, but we need more.

Over recent years, we have seen some progress in this area. We are starting to become more public relations conscious, but we have to become professional about it.

It's really important folks.

We have the best case. Let's get the best public relations strategy to get our message out.

Freedom of Speech

In the Arab World, the concept of freedom of speech is an oxymoron. It doesn't exist as a free entity at all.

It is dominated by control that is founded on age.

The leader is not selected on the basis of skills and experience, but on age, the simplest form of experience and the least effective.

Our leaders were the aged and the mentally limited. Tradition dictated their actions, not reality or strategy.

We fought against what we knew, yet we knew little about the West and the powers that lay behind the strength of the Jewish settlers who came to Palestine in the thousands.

The media portrayed us as the vagrants, the thieves, the cutthroats. Image and perception has a lot to do with motivation.

We had no perception.

Our image was defined by control, not freedom of choice. Arabs feared free thought, because free thought undermined the concept of our system of leadership.

Of 22 Arab countries, every one of them is controlled by a dictator, a monarchy or a military regime. Democracy existed only as one point on a professed revolutionary agenda.

Without free speech, we had no real media. Only propaganda. And the propagandist's role is to lead the people into believing that which is not possible.

Today, there is some movement forward. We have advocacy journalism in the Middle East and Arab countries. But it is still limited free speech.

Freedom of thought undermines the power of the dictator.

The media in a military state is a government controlled system of lies and distortions intended to bend reality.

That self-inflicted hallucination allowed us to be overcome in 1948 by a ragtag, but better equipped army of more determined civilians who fought as individuals in a community, rather than as conscripts against their will.

So in 1948, as the Jewish people declared their country and the British army departed from the shores of Palestine through Haifa, the Palestinian people lived in the false comfort that the great armies of the Arab World would come to their defense.

They did not.

Armies of failure trailed into our country as the Jewish Haganah and Palmach carefully staked out their nation.

The greatness of the armies was an image fed to us by our Arab leaders, a false image. Idols of lies. We sat back, and before we knew it, we were chased from our homes. Masses of refugees fled the reality that our leaders had carefully hid from our eyes.

Emotion and lies described the "Jew" who took our homes.

And they had to preserve that lie that it was the Jew who stole our homes, rather than that our leadership gave us away.

In the years that followed *Al Nakba* in 1948, we saw continued incidents of failure. The leadership of the Arab World had to protect its great secret, that they had failed. Israel was not as victorious as we had been a great failure.

And it was punishment for a Palestinian gunman to assassinate the leader of this great hoax, King Abdullah, as he prayed at the steps of the Al Aqsa Mosque in a Jordanian controlled Jerusalem. He would never release that city to the Palestinians, and some said he was a collaborator with our defeat.

In the years to come, the leadership of the Arab World, through their controlled media, painted a picture of the wicked Israel.

Some of their crimes were accurate. But accuracy was never enough for the Arab masses. The crimes of Israel had to be exaggerated even more to cover up for the inadequacies of the Arab World leadership. How could we admit that we had failed?

In Syria today, one of the so-called "Confrontation States," a computer modem is still as illegal as a drug.

The modem is the symbol of free thought and communication.

In 1967, we were again told that the Arab Leadership would redeem the honor of the Arab World and recapture Palestine.

It was one of the greatest hoaxes that allowed Egypt's President Gamal Abdul Nasser to lie to his people that the great Armies of Egypt would come to liberate Palestine. His intentions were sincere, but his intentions were founded on falsehoods.

As he stood at the microphone of his control talking hyperbole to his people, Israel's reality stormed across the Sinai and into Egypt. Syria's "army" collapsed in minutes of each contact with Israel's tanks in the Golan Heights, and Jordan's ego shattered just as quickly.

The Six Day War is a horror of the greatest magnitude, a nightmare of reality of the Arab people and for Palestinians.

It caused the Palestinians, for the first time, to awaken and to muster for themselves a defense.

In this failure was born a Palestinian movement to fight for its own freedom. Pent up anger in the Palestinians directed this force to embrace terrorism. Striking at the easy targets. Blowing up airplanes in the desert. Murdering innocent civilians who were easier targets than the Israeli military which was better trained and better equipped.

Some argue that the turn toward terrorism was forced upon the Palestinians by a Western society that denied Palestinians and Arabs equal representation in the media or in political discourse.

Our leadership was ill equipped to lead. It still is.

In our culture, the leader is not selected because of his education or skills, but on the basis of seniority and age.

Those who are the more skilled leaders are often undermined, disgraced, humiliated or killed by those who rule by emotion in order to control the masses.

We owed our loyalty and allegiance to the wisdom of our fathers.

Women had no ranking in Arabian society, yet the Arab world

was dominated by the emotion of women and the tall tales of wives. In 1948, Arab honor refused to accept the reality that we could not defeat Jewish settlers backed by the power of the West.

While the world saw the plight of the Jews through the eyes of the media, we did not understand what the media was and neither did we recognize its significant impact on the world's opinion and on our own futures.

We had no media.

We had no freedom.

We could never have victory.

Today, there is a serious movement toward peace.

It may not last. It could come to a halt.

Ironically, it is the Palestinians who have changed and have, for thefirst time agreed to negotiate a compromise with israel.

And, it is Israel who shows reluctance to make peace with the Palestinians, still clinging to the lost hope that it can divide the Arab World, conclude partial peace agreements with Egypt, Jordan and Syria, and preserve a no-war, no-peace status quo.

But that status quo cannot last. And, in the end, time is on our side.

The Jewish people are great teachers of history and politics.

They taught us that they waited 2,000 years to Return to Palestine and re-establish their state.

We don't want to wait 2,000 years.

But if the Palestinian people must, they will.

About The Author

Ray Hanania is an awardwinning former Chicago political reporter and journalist who cut his teeth covering the mayoral administrations of Richard J. Daley, Michael A. Bilandic, Jane M. Byrne, Harold Washington, David Orr, Eugene Sawyer and Richard M. Daley, as a freelancer and as City Hall reporter for the *Daily Southtown Economist* and the Chicago *Sun-Times* newspapers.

He has received numerous honors and awards including a nomination for a Pulitzer Prize by the Chicago *Sun-Times* in 1991 for the series of stories included in this book about life in the West Bank. And, he was awarded the prestigious Peter Lisagor/Sigma Delta Chi Award for Column writing in 1985. He twice received the Chicago Newspaper Guild's Stick-O-Type Award for column writing.

Mr. Hanania is the former Publisher of *The Villager Newspapers*, distributed in the southwest suburbs of Chicago. His humor columns appear in each issue, addressing a wide range of topics.

An activist for peace between Israel and the Palestinians, Mr. Hanania has served as the first National President of the Palestinian American Congress, as spokesman for the former Arab American Congress for Palestine, as an officer of the Arab American Anti-Discrimination Committee, and as an Executive Board member of the Arab American Institute. He served as president of the National Association of Arab American Journalists, and as publisher of *The Middle Eastern Voice* English-language newspaper. His writings advocating a peaceful resolution of the Middle East conflict have appeared in many Arab and American publications in the United States.

This is his first published novel.

If you would like information on how you can order
more copies of this book or future books and publications by Ray
Hanania, please contact:

Urban Strategies Group Publishing Inc.
PO Box 356
Tinley Park, IL 60477

708-403-3380
FAX: 708-403-3380

E-Mail: **rhanania@theramp.net**

World Wide Web: **http://www.usg.org**

Free Computer Bulletin Board System: 708-429-0553